The
Hijaz Railroad

THE
HIJAZ
RAILROAD

William Ochsenwald

University Press of Virginia
Charlottesville

The publication of this volume is sponsored by the VPI Educational
Foundation, Inc.

THE UNIVERSITY PRESS OF VIRGINIA
Copyright © 1980 by the Rector and Visitors
of the University of Virginia

First published 1980

Library of Congress Cataloging in Publication Data

Ochsenwald, William.
    The Hijaz Railroad.

    Bibliography: p.
    Includes index.
    1. Hejaz Railway.   I. Title.
HE3390.H4025   385'.0956   8010505
ISBN 0813908256

Printed in the United States of America

CONTENTS

TABLES

MAPS

PREFACE

While reading about or seeing enacted the dramatic history of
the Arab Revolt against the Ottoman Empire during World War
I and the experiences of Lawrence of Arabia, millions of people
have come into contact with the destruction of the Hijaz Railroad. The other side of the coin, the story of the railroad from
the Ottoman point of view, remains to be told. Beneath the ro-
mance of the years when empires fell and new states and heroes
arose there is a more sober but equally important story: the functioning of institutions.

When riding the Hijaz Railroad between Damascus and
Maan, one sees everywhere remnants of the Ottoman period of
control. These reminders of the Ottoman past seem to imply by
their presence that other sources of information on the railroad
may be equally durable. Yet my search for written information
about the railroad showed that the materials for its history have
been less lasting than its rails, freight cars, and stations: the
sources for Ottoman and Arab institutional history are less
abundant and more difficult to find than those dealing with the
more dramatic military history.

The fate of the railroad's records illustrates the nature of problems encountered in historical research in the Middle East. The
collapse of imperial rule in the Arab lands in 1918 probably
caused the loss of the major source of information on the history
of the railroad. The Damascus records of the railroad are simply
missing. Interviews in 1970 with Hijaz Railroad officials in Damascus and Amman and with the director of the committee for
the restoration of the Hijaz Railroad support the claim made in

1924 by the "Representative of Syria who stated that the archives of the railroad in Damascus had been destroyed and that
it was impossible to [find them]."[1] Luckily, the railroad itself
published a number of its own records, now available in Istanbul
libraries. These include detailed financial accounts and guides to
the railroad's administration. There also are numerous papers of
the central administration in the Istanbul Başbakanlık Arşivi, the
Prime Ministry Archives.

   In the absence of the railroad's local archives it is necessary to
piece together information from a number of sources, extracting
data from works that were not written with the railroad as the
center of the writer's concern. The British and French Foreign
Ministry archives are the chief sources of information which contain occasional data on the railroad. The difficulty of squeezing
out facts from divergent material is compounded by two problems: the carelessness of foreign observers and Ottoman censor-
ship, which limited local writers' criticism. The validity of Ottoman governmental reports and European diplomatic records
can at times be checked by comparison with contemporary pe-
riodicals, memoirs, and travel accounts.

   Certain types of sources pertain only to limited areas of the
railroad's history. The studies of the railroad written by German
engineers who worked in Syria provide a good deal of information on construction though relatively little on other aspects of
the railroad, such as operations and financing. Interviews with
railroad employees or their descendants give some data on the
conditions of workers and construction crews. However, oral
evidence is overlain with sixty years of experience of the Hijaz
Railroad under non-Ottoman control.

   Since the end of World War I, there have been only four books
that attempt to overcome the difficulties presented by the railroad's historical sources. The broadest of these is the published
doctoral dissertation of Eleuthère Eleftériadès, vice president of
the Damas, Hama et Prolongements Railroad (D.H.P.).
Eleftériadès made full use of the D.H.P.'s records and French

---

[1] Eugène Borel, *Répartition des annuités de la dette publique ottomane* (Geneva:
A. Kundig, 1925), p. 89.

archives but was unable to consult Ottoman materials. He deals chiefly with the history of the D.H.P. Ahmad al-Marawani's geographical thesis spends relatively little time on the history of the railroad but does contain a number of useful observations on the topography of the line and the problems of construction. James K. Holman's study, the only general examination of the railroad to appear in English, is limited almost entirely to Western sources. The book that Jacob M. Landau edited has a useful introduction to the history of the railroad. Most of the book is a translation of an Arabic appeal to build the railroad and a description of the pilgrimage before construction began.[2] These four works do not discuss in detail such key problems as its social impact, its financing, and the use of foreign personnel in key technical posts.

A work that is highly valuable for its insights into British policy in the Hijaz, the dissertation of Saleh Muhammad Al-Amr, although it does not deal with the railroad in depth, nevertheless has been of considerable utility in dealing with the background to this study.[3]

The value of having a work that talks about all aspects of the Hijaz Railroad's history perhaps compensates for the inevitably provisional character of its conclusions. The nature of the Ottoman reaction to Western imperialism can perhaps be illuminated even by a tentative study of the only railroad the empire constructed, paid for, and operated.

In addition to sources there is the perpetual problem of transliteration. I feel that it is of major importance in the names of individuals and the titles of sources; in these Arabic is transliterated according to the system used in the journal *Arabian Studies*, with some slight modifications. However, all diacritical marks have been eliminated except for the 'ayn. Ottoman words are

---

[2] Eleftériadès, *Les chemins de fer en Syrie et au Liban* (Beirut: Imprimerie Catholique, 1944); al-Marawani, *Al-Khatt al-hadidi al-hijazi* (Damascus: Damascus Univ., 1959); Holman, "Sacred Line to Madina: The History of the Hejaz Railway," A.B. thesis, Princeton, 1967; Landau, *The Hejaz Railway and the Muslim Pilgrimage* (Detroit: Wayne State Univ. Press, 1971).

[3] Saleh Muhammad Al-Amr, "The Hijaz under Ottoman rule, 1869–1914," Diss., Univ. of Leeds, 1974.

spelled according to current Turkish usage. Authors' spellings of
their own names in Western alphabets have been retained when
citing works written in languages other than Arabic or Ottoman.
Most place-names are presented according to the spelling
adopted by the *Times Atlas of the World*, except for the omission
of signs for 'ayns, alifs, and ta marbutahs from place-names.

A careful analysis of the value of Ottoman money in the different parts of the empire at the beginning of the twentieth century is not yet available. The value of the Ottoman pound (T.L.)
even in terms of Ottoman coins flucuated from year to year and
from place to place. For purposes of convenience in making com-
parisons, unless otherwise noted, it is assumed that T.L. equals
100 kuruş. The smallest denomination of Ottoman coin, the
para, is not included in any numbers. The price structure and
the purchasing power of Ottoman currency are similarly unstu-
died, at least for the Arab provinces. A brief indication of some
salaries and wages is included in chapter 3 in an attempt to give
a context for the contributions made to the railroad. All foreign
money is stated in terms of its Ottoman equivalent.

A number of institutions and individuals opened their facilities
for research, made information available, and provided valuable
criticism. My research in the Middle East in 1969–70 was made
possible by a Fulbright-Hays grant. In addition to those formerly associated with the railroad or their relatives who granted
me interviews, the staffs of the Public Record Office, Ministère
des Affaires Etrangères, the Başbakanlık Arşivi, the Belediye
and Istanbul University libraries, and the Library of the American University in Beirut were most helpful.

In addition I acknowledge with gratitude the help of Suleiman
Mousa, Halil İnalcik, Eleuthère Eleftériadès, Jibran Bikhazi,
Bernard Lewis, and George Chadwick. The comments on different parts of the manuscript by Bernie Lalor, Butros Abu
Manneh, R. B. Serjeant, Robin Bidwell, R. Bayley Winder, and
Albert Kudsi-Zadeh were most welcome. I wish especially to
thank Jacob Landau and Robert Landen for their many helpful
criticisms. The editors of *The Muslim World* and *Die Welt des Islams*
have kindly given permission to reprint sections of chapters 5

and 3, which originally appeared in different form in those journals. Dr. William Mackie, head of the Department of History at Virginia Polytechnic Institute, helped provide financial assistance for the preparation of the maps. Professor Richard Hoffman, chairman of the University Press Committee at V.P.I., helped secure funds to enable publication of this work.

Hijaz Railroad authorities in Jordan displayed great hospitality in permitting me to inspect the southern parts of the railroad; shoveling coal on a freight train from Amman to Maan certainly provided a new perspective on the history of the railroad. My thanks also go to the University of Riyadh, which enabled me to see the northern Hijaz in 1977. The reception of the people of al-Ula was overwhelming.

Professors Richard Chambers and Fahir İz aided in the preparation of this work by their comments and advice. Their thoughtfulness and help in Chicago and Istanbul, respectively, were invaluable. During five years at the University of Chicago I benefited from the encouragement, criticism, and guidance provided by William R. Polk. I thank him for the training I have received from him. Sydney Fisher of the Ohio State University has, by example and friendship, provided me with a constant source of inspiration.

The photographs that illustrate the text were taken for Sultan Abdülhamid II in the 1900s. Copies were made and are here reproduced with the kind permission of the Istanbul University Library.

Ultimately this book owes most to the members of my family and my friends, in particular my aunt, Mrs. Barbara Kaiser, and my grandfather, William Ochsenwald.

ABBREVIATIONS

AB	Great Britain. Foreign Office 882/25–28, *The Arab Bulletin*.
BBA-Defter	Turkey. Başbakanlık Arşivi. Yıldız. 36. 140/66. 140. XXIII.
D.H.P.	Damas, Hama et Prolongements Railroad
Donor's List	*Thamarat al-Funun*, Tammuz 1900.
Durham	University of Durham. School of Oriental Studies. Sudan Archives, "Reports and papers relating to the Hijaz Railway."
F	France. Ministère des Affaires Etrangères. Turquie. Politique intérieure: Syrie, Liban
FIP	France. Ministère des Affaires Etrangères. Indes.
F.O.	Great Britain. Foreign Office.
FP	France. Ministère des Affaires Etrangères. Turquie. Politique intérieure: Palestine.
FPM	France. Ministère des Affaires Etrangères. Turquie. Politique intérieure: Arabie-Yemen—Pèlerinage.
FRA	France. Ministère des Affaires Etrangères. Turquie. Chemins de fer.
FY	France. Ministère des Affaires Etrangères. Turquie. Politique intérieure: Arabie-Yemen, 1896–1914.
HD	[Hijaz Railroad]. *Hicaz Demiryolunun Varidat*, *1330*.
HD–7	[Hijaz Railroad]. *Hicaz Demiryolunun 1327 Senesi Istatistik Rapor*.
HDL	[Hijaz Railroad]. *Hicaz Demiryolu Layıhası*.

HVA-M	[Hijaz Railroad]. *Hicaz ve Süriye*.
Int. Res.	International Resources Engineering and Exploration Group. *Design Report*.
IO	India Office Archives. "Arabia: the Hedjaz Railway."
MKA-SAH 1	Muhammad Kurd 'Ali. "Sikkat al-Hijaz." *Al-Muqtataf*.
TF	*Thamarat al-Funun* (Beirut). The following abbreviations are used for months in *TF*: January, K al-Th; October, T al-A; November, T al-Th; December, K al-A.

The
Hijaz Railroad

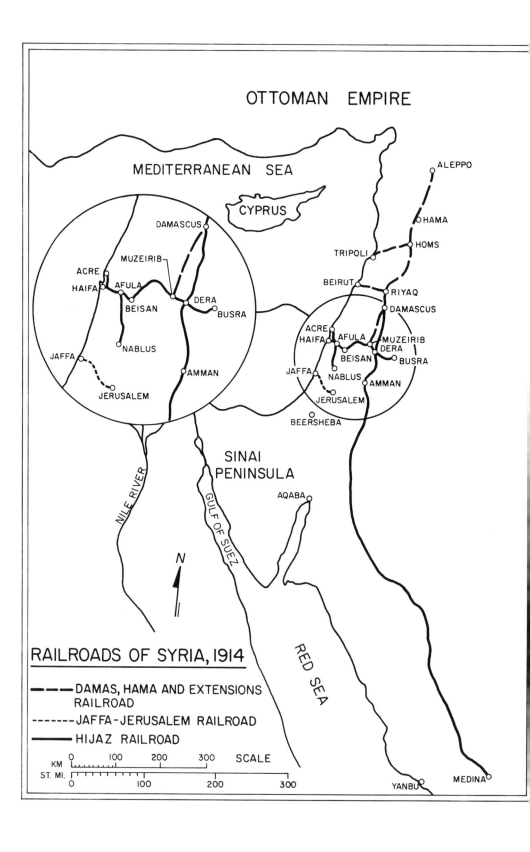

OTTOMAN EMPIRE

MEDITERRANEAN SEA

ALEPPO

CYPRUS

DAMASCUS

HAMA

MUZEIRIB

HOMS

TRIPOLI

ACRE

AFULA

BEIRUT

RIYAQ

HAIFA

BEISAN

DERA

DAMASCUS

BUSRA

ACRE

HAIFA

AFULA

MUZEIRIB

NABLUS

DERA

BEISAN

BUSRA

JAFFA

JAFFA

NABLUS

AMMAN

AMMAN

JERUSALEM

JERUSALEM

BEERSHEBA

SINAI
PENINSULA

NILE RIVER

AQABA

GULF OF SUEZ

N

RED SEA

RAILROADS OF SYRIA, 1914

— — — DAMAS, HAMA AND EXTENSIONS
RAILROAD

------- JAFFA-JERUSALEM RAILROAD

——— HIJAZ RAILROAD

KM 0   100   200   300   SCALE

ST. MI. 0   100   200   300

YANBU

MEDINA

Chapter I

Introduction

THE HIJAZ RAILROAD stands out starkly against the desert land-
scape of South Syria and Jordan, a reminder of the Ottoman
imperial past in the midst of the Arab present.[1] It is a symbol of
an attempt to resist European control and influence. Before the
territories of Syria, Jordan, and Palestine came into existence at
the behest of Britain and France, the Ottoman Empire in the
1900s and 1910s made in this area one last attempt at revival.
Bankrupt, defeated in war, dependent upon foreign investment,
the Ottomans tried to take the initiative in order to gain independence from European technical tutelage and to counter the growing threat of European armies. While the rest of the empire's

---

[1] The term *Syria* when not otherwise qualified refers to the areas included
as of 1978 in the countries of Syria, Lebanon, Jordan, and Israel. The vilayet
of Syria in 1900 was bounded in the south by Aqaba, on the east by the Syrian
desert, on the west by the Beqa Valley and the Jordan, and on the north by
the vilayet of Aleppo. "South Syria" is limited to Syria south of Damascus,
Jordan, and Palestine south of Jerusalem.

transportation network had been built by Europeans, this line would be financed, constructed, and operated by Ottomans.

It was a massive undertaking for an empire inexperienced in operating its own public utilities. Large sums of money had to be raised while the empire was near bankruptcy. Construction and operation involved the efficient organizing of the efforts of thousands of men and the movement of hundreds of tons of freight and material. Once the line was built, the new political and military limits of Ottoman influence had to be established in South Syria and the Hijaz.

How the Ottomans went about achieving increased political control and autonomy despite their weakness will be examined by looking at problems as different from one another as that of hiring European personnel or using Ottoman methods of telling time. Beneath the varying techniques and approaches used in the Hijaz Railroad project there were common themes of intent and will that united them. The leadership of the Ottoman central government intensely desired the railroad because of the events that had caused Ottoman weakness during the nineteenth century.

The Ottoman Empire had initially attempted to contain European imperialism by increasing its military capability without making major changes in other aspects of society. Only those institutions directly related to innovations were to be altered. The political process, the goals of the bureaucracy and the rulers, and existing economic and social relationships could continue to change in familiar ways. Russian victories over the Ottomans in 1828 and the destruction of the Ottoman-Egyptian fleet at Navarino showed that the two main military powers of the Middle East remained inferior to European power. It became clear that more far-reaching reforms were needed to create the military and political strength to meet the European challenge. The simple borrowing of techniques of organization in the army and the purchase of war matériel had resulted in some improvement of Ottoman strength, but the central government would have to mobilize the loyalty of those people who had been only nominally subject to the state. In the meantime larger standing armies made an increase in revenues necessary. Simultaneous with the expansion and reform of the army in the central area of the Ottoman Empire, symbolized by the destruction of the Janissaries in 1826, an expansion of conscription and taxation into formerly autonomous areas was initiated. While such rulers as Mahmud II and Mehmet Ali of Egypt gathered power into their own hands, the central government began to spread its power to the provinces.

At the same time that Egypt and the Ottoman Empire undertook to raise large armies and navies in the 1820s and 1830s, technological discoveries in Europe provided new methods of increasing military capacity. Chief among these was the railroad.

When non-European states sought to construct railroads, they were forced by lack of capital, personnel, and experience to allow European companies to assume control of the projects. Ottoman railroads were nearly all controlled and built by foreigners. Railroads managed by foreigners were built and operated in such a way that the penetration of the internal economy by European economic interests took place.

During the Tanzimat period (1839–76) the Ottoman Empire was brought into the European capital market; Ottoman bonds were sold in European exchanges and European capitalists invested in Ottoman public works. Economic subservience to Western Europe was added to the European military superiority that had existed since the early nineteenth century. If the empire was to survive, there was a need for an independent initiative that would not be just another response to a specific European challenge. The ability of the empire to meet foreign encroachment and control internal revolts depended on its planning and implementing methods of centralization and gaining in military force. These goals could be achieved only by Ottoman action, planned to meet Ottoman needs, not by piecemeal reactions to individual European acts of aggression. Yet the Ottoman Empire was faced with nearly insurmountable difficulties that often came simultaneously, making planning and initiative difficult for the burdened central government.

For Sultan Abdülhamid II (r. 1876–1909) the difficulty of formulating a coherent response to Western imperialism was made even more of a problem by his fear of the political consequences

4 The Hijaz Railroad

of modernization. Like other rulers who faced the same problem around the turn of the century, such as Czar Nicholas II in Russia, he recognized the danger of radical innovation to the bases of his support. Abdülhamid sought to use the existing forces of religion and Islamic solidarity to reinforce the traditions of rule as exercised by the Ottoman royal dynasty in the past. He rejected Western imperialism, nationalism, liberalism, and constitutionalism. He nevertheless sought to use Western technology to pursue the goals of centralization and independence. The epitome of the Hamidian method to achieve traditional goals and oppose Western values was the Hijaz Railroad.

Ottoman Weakness and European Expansion

Ottoman weakness in the face of European expansion was obvious as early as the reign of Sultan Mahmud II (1808–39). Military defeats by European armies such as that leading to the loss of the Crimea and successful insurrections of subject peoples as in Serbia had occurred during the late eighteenth and early nineteenth centuries. These losses were somewhat compensated during Mahmud's reign and that of his immediate successors when the central government regained effective control over the nearly autonomous local notables of the European and Anatolian provinces. Under Mahmud the minimal goals of the state were achieved. Thanks to the aid of the anti-French coalition of European powers, the Arabic-speaking lands that Mehmet Ali of Egypt had gained were restored in 1840. In the ensuing years of the Tanzimat security was established, garrisons of Ottoman troops gained military superiority over local forces, and a beginning was made on regularizing and centralizing conscription and taxation.

Building the military strength needed to achieve centralization and reforming the central bureaucracy taxed the financial and military resources of the Ottoman Empire to the limit. At the same time, the principles upon which the state operated were under attack: the position of the sultan as a decision maker without responsibility to an elective body was opposed by liberals, while the political value attached to religion, culture, dynasty, and tradition was questioned by nationalists. In the middle of the 1870s all of the various pressures threatening the empire coalesced to produce a crisis.

In 1875–77 the Ottoman Empire went through financial bankruptcy and was defeated by Russian troops who came close to Istanbul. A coup d'etat brought about the proclamation of a written constitution with an elected parliament. After the short reign of Sultan Murad V (1876), a new ruler was placed on the throne by the top civil bureaucrats who controlled the central government.

Abdülhamid II's thirty-two-year reign was based on five principal points of change from the preceding Tanzimat era: (1) personal rule, (2) Pan-Islam, (3) reform of the army to modernize it without liberalizing the officer corps, (4) maintenance of financial independence from Europe by refusing to seek loans, and (5) an unwritten alliance with at least one European Power.[2] All five had a close connection with the Hijaz Railroad project. Autocratic rule allowed it to be successfully pushed through the sluggish Ottoman bureaucracy. The Pan-Islamic movement helped in obtaining money. Military modernization was partially dependent upon more rapid mobilization and troop movement. Financial autarchy was a prerequisite to control of Ottoman utilities. The German-controlled Baghdad Railroad, which was to be Syria's link to Anatolia and Istanbul, received the enthusiastic support of the German government.

Abdülhamid immediately set out to reverse the challenges posed to his control over the state and to begin to rescue the empire from its foreign dangers. While he succeeded in the first six years of his reign in maneuvering the Tanzimat bureaucrats out of power and installing his own supporters in key posts, he

[2] For the best general discussion of the Hamidian period, see Stanford J. Shaw and Ezel Kural Shaw, *History of the Ottoman Empire and Modern Turkey* (Cambridge: Cambridge Univ. Pres, 1977), II, 172–271; for a brief but incisive analysis of Abdülhamid's responses to nationalism, see Roderic Davison, "Nationalism as an Ottoman Problem and the Ottoman Response," in William Haddad and William Ochsenwald, eds., *Nationalism in a Non-National State* (Columbus: Ohio State Univ. Press, 1977), pp. 25–56.

was forced to agree to loss of territory in Europe and the creation of European economic control over the empire's debt.

The first of his goals was personal political power. The Hamidian regime evolved into a tightly centralized autocracy that was avowedly antiliberal and antinationalist. Parliament was dissolved; new elections were not held until 1908. Abdülhamid felt that cultural nationalism was antithetical to Ottoman unity. An application of national self-determination would divide the empire into small states. Because Abdülhamid recaptured political power from the bureaucrats, all major decisions had to be made at the Court and most by the sultan himself. Once he had gained this authority he was capable of forcing the slow-moving Ottoman bureaucracy to undertake action rapidly. A network of spies and detailed reports kept the bureaucracy under close observation.

The second part of Abdülhamid's program involved the creation of an ideology that would mobilize his subjects for active support of his regime.

Ottoman political loyalty in the past had depended upon those Muslims who participated in Ottoman culture. The Ottomans were few; in the provinces they consisted chiefly of the office-holding elite and local notables. The empire was so diverse in culture and so separated geographically by poor transportation that in the past only this political elite, which circulated through it, had linked its separate parts together.

The Ottoman elite had failed to overcome separatist movements in Europe; some continued to plague Abdülhamid. Crete, Macedonia, and Armenians in Anatolia were rebellious. While an increase in military might was needed merely to maintain the empire in its present frontiers, there was also the need for new policies if the empire was to be able to prevent such outbreaks from occurring in the future. A method had to be found to expand the appeal of being an Ottoman to larger groups of subjects. Abdülhamid found only one force that would not disrupt the nature of his rule: the emotional strength attached to his position of caliph.

The Pan-Islamic policy and its attendant propaganda as adopted by the sultan were designed to achieve two goals: to gain the support of foreign Muslims throughout the world for the Ottoman Empire and to increase Ottoman Sunni loyalty to his rule. A heightened feeling of identity with the Ottoman Empire by the Muslims of the European colonial possessions might affect their loyalty to their Christian rulers. Millions of Muslims in India and North Africa might be induced to rebel. The threat of being able to turn on or off the danger of religious rebellion could persuade the European nations with Muslim colonies to adopt a pro-Ottoman foreign policy. The British and French foreign archives reflect European concern with the dangers posed by a successful Ottoman exploitation of Pan-Islamic sentiment.

Pan-Islam as expounded by Jamal al-Din al-Afghani was purely an ideological movement that did not provide any way by which large numbers of Ottoman subjects or other Muslims could participate in it.[3] The campaign for donations to the Hijaz Railroad was the first instance when a specific Pan-Islamic project involving mass participation could be encouraged by the empire.

The third point in Abdülhamid's reform plans was military reform and modernization following European models. If the sultan's centralization of power and his Pan-Islamic projects were to be realized, the army had to become strong enough to defend the empire. The sultan realized that peace was a prerequisite to military reform.[4] The military reforms were based on the allocation of much of the state's income to the army. About one-half of total Ottoman income between 1886 and 1895 was spent on the armed forces.[5] The outlay, although it taxed the empire's budget to the breaking point, yielded only limited

[3] For a discussion of al-Afghani's vision of Pan-Islam, see three works of Nikki R. Keddie: "Pan-Islam as Proto-Nationalism," *Journal of Modern History*, 41 (1969), 17–28; *An Islamic Response to Imperialism* (Berkeley: Univ. of California Press, 1968); *Sayyid Jamal ad-Din "al-Afghani"* (Berkeley: Univ. of California Press, 1972).

[4] Abdülhamid said, "No other country has a greater need for peace and tranquillity than our Empire" (Ali Vahbi Bey, comp., *Avant la débacle de la Turquie* [Paris: Attinger frères, 1922], p. 77).

[5] Merwin A. Griffiths, "The Reorganization of the Ottoman Army under Abdülhamid II, 1880–1897," Diss., Univ. of California, Los Angeles, 1966, p. 181.

benefits. The Greek-Ottoman War of 1897 ended in an Ottoman victory, but in the Italian and Balkan wars of 1911–14 the empire lost extensive territory in Europe and North Africa. The modernization of the army was limited to better training for officers and purchasing equipment from Europe.

Foreign trading missions helped the Ottoman Army to reorganize. After the Revolution of 1908 and the coming to power of the Committee of Union and Progress (C.U.P.), German influence in the army, which had been strong earlier, increased. The Ottomans remained dependent on foreign suppliers for artillery and war vessels.

A number of small-scale mutinies indicated that soldiers were not being paid. In Beirut in 1901, 1,300 troops mutinied for ten months' back pay. In Damascus in December 1902 about 100 officers seized a telegraph office and cabled the sultan, demanding their arrears be paid. They were told by officials in Istanbul that there were no funds to pay them.[6] Salaries were low and were irregularly paid when given at all. Conscripts were kept beyond the time when they should have been discharged. Deaths among troops in the Arab provinces were especially high because of bad sanitation, poor military health facilities, and difficult conditions of service.

Although with the exception of the Greek War there were no formal external conflicts during Abdülhamid's reign, after 1891 there was nearly continual warfare in Yemen. Major uprisings took place in 1891 and 1904; by 1905 the capital city of the vilayet had been lost to the rebels. Under the Imam Yahya the highlands of Yemen remained effectively independent of Ottoman control even during periods of relative peace. Poor military transportation on land was overcome only by sending troops to Yemen by sea. Naval communication with Yemen depended upon the Suez Canal, which could be closed at the will of the English, who controlled Egypt. The troops sent to Yemen feared going there so greatly that they occasionally mutinied even before reaching their destination. Syrian reservists en route to Yemen revolted in 1903 while in transit through the Suez Canal.

6 F, 108, Savoye (Damascus) to Delcassé, 3 December 1902.

They were subsequently diverted to working on the Hijaz Railroad.[7]

The way in which the Yemeni revolts could be permanently crushed was to gain military superiority, which depended to a considerable extent on improving transportation of troops and matériel to the area of fighting. The success enjoyed by the Ottomans in the Greek War because of troop mobilization on the Thessaloniki-Constantinople Railroad demonstrated that railroads could provide the needed increment of military strength to defeat the enemy.[8] Once the Hijaz Railroad came close to the Red Sea, it would speed transportation. After it reached Mecca it could be extended toward Yemen.

The fourth major area of change in Sultan Abdülhamid's program to restore Ottoman political and military strength was financial. Money for reforms was limited by the allocation of much of the empire's income to the Ottoman Public Debt Administration (O.P.D.A.). Since the O.P.D.A. was under foreign control, first priority was given to debt repayment: interest on the foreign debt was reduced to a level the empire could afford to pay and the principal was gradually reduced.[9]

Foreign borrowing by the state meant the pledging of specific revenues as guarantees. These revenues were then assigned to the O.P.D.A. for collection. Although Abdülhamid agreed to do this for the Baghdad Railway financing, he preferred to avoid it. Since there was no budget surplus in most years, the chief way to gain new funds was to raise the customs rate on imports. In order to do this the consent of all the European powers was necessary. To get all of the powers to agree meant endless concessions to each of them, as was demonstrated in the tariff negotiations of the 1900s.

Additional taxes, at least in the Arab territories, were likely

[7] F, 109, Sercey (Beirut) to Delcassé, 18 May 1903.

[8] Clive Bigham, Viscount Mersey, *With the Turkish Army in Thessaly* (London: Macmillan, 1897), p. 12; Louis Rambert, *Notes et Impressions de Turquie* (Geneva: Ator, 1926), pp. 62–63.

[9] Donald C. Blaisdell, *European Financial Control in the Ottoman Empire* (New York: Columbia Univ. Press, 1929); Herbert Feis, *Europe, the World's Banker, 1870–1914* (New Haven: Yale Univ. Press, 1930), pp. 313–17.

either to be evaded or to cause revolts. Major expenditures on
new items of reform seemed impossible when the empire frequently could not meet even government salaries, much less pay
bills due.[10]

The last way Abdülhamid tried to overcome the weakness of
the empire was his securing of an informal alliance with one of
the European powers, Germany. By the late 1890s the Ottomans
had seen their chief economic investor, France, ally itself with
Russia, their most persistent enemy. Both Russian expansionism
in Asia and the growth of Bulgaria, its chief ally in the Balkans,
were at the expense of the Ottoman Empire. A former ally, Britain, had occupied Cyprus and Egypt in the early years of
Abdülhamid's reign. In 1899 Britain and the ruler of Kuwait
entered into an agreement that guaranteed British support of
Kuwait's autonomy while reserving for Britain control of Kuwait's external relations. Britain opposed construction of a German-controlled railroad to Basra or Kuwait because Britain
feared the extension of German-Ottoman military power closer
to the Persian Gulf and India. Another source of Ottoman-Brit-
ish disagreement was the undelimited Yemen-Aden frontier.
Only Germany among the major powers of Europe was left, for
it and Austria-Hungary did not join the powers in opposing the
empire on such issues as Macedonian reform, the handling of the
Cretan insurrections, and the Armenian massacres.

The German emperor William II visited Istanbul in 1889 and
again in 1898. On the latter journey he also visited Jerusalem
and Damascus. Although other countries continued to provide
the bulk of foreign loans, some governmental and military advisers, and external trade, Germany's role was increasing in all
three areas throughout the 1890s and 1900s.

The single German project that most caught the attention of
Europe was the Baghdad Railroad. Intended to connect the existing West Anatolian railroads with Southeastern Anatolia,
Aleppo, Baghdad, and the Persian Gulf, this railroad was seen
as a means of gaining German economic and military preponder-
ance in the areas traversed. Ottoman goals of political centrali-

[10] Rambert, *Notes*, p. 14.

zation and economic development could also be met while there at the same time was an implied threat to British hegemony in the gulf.[11]

Overall foreign control of the economy, no matter what the source, increased under Abdülhamid and his successors until World War I. Even nominally Ottoman companies were really owned and controlled by foreigners. The major railroads, banks, port facilities, gas and water works, streetcar companies, and some mines were foreign controlled.[12]

Two Provinces as Examples of Ottoman Weakness
South Syria and the Hijaz

In seeking to increase Ottoman military capacity, political centralization, and economic autarchy, Mahmud II and the Tanzimat leaders had directed prime attention to reforms in Istanbul, Rumelia, and Anatolia. Once the semiautonomous areas of North and Central Iraq and Syria had been brought into the Ottoman system of taxation and conscription, they were subsequently ignored. Parts of these areas (e.g., the Druze territory in Syria) retained their autonomy even after this time. It was only in the cities and towns that Ottoman military forces ensured order. The process of disaffection that helped create a national, cultural, and religious opposition to Ottoman rule in the European provinces was largely unknown among the Muslims of the Syrian and Hijazi towns. It was only in Mount Lebanon that separatism, social changes, and emigration caused anti-Ottoman activism, stemming originally from the massacres of 1860 and Christian-Muslim antagonism. The vast majority of Muslims were either passive or favored only more autonomy, remaining loyal to the empire until the middle or end of World War I.[13]

---

[11] For a full discussion of German railroad building and its economic and political impact upon the Ottoman Empire, see Donald Quataert, "Ottoman Reform and Agriculture in Anatolia, 1876–1908," Diss., Univ. of California, Los Angeles, 1973.

[12] Kurt Wiedenfeld, *Die deutsch-türkischen Wirtschaftsbeziehungen und ihre Entwicklungsmöglichkeiten* (Munich: Duncker, 1915), pp. 31 ff.

[13] Arab nationalist organizations were small and relatively late in organizing compared to other linguistic groups. The Turkification process in education

The position of the Arabic-speaking peoples within the empire became more important as the European parts of it decreased in size. Some Arabs had always been brought into the Ottoman elite through assimilation to Ottoman culture, education, and officeholding in the provinces. However, the number of high officials in the empire of Arab origin before Abdülhamid II had been low. When he gained the throne in 1876, a conscious policy of promoting Arabs to high offices was begun.[14]

Some of Abdülhamid's closest advisers were Arabs. 'Izzat Paşa al-'Abid, the sultan's second secretary and chief adviser in the late 1890s and 1900s, was from Damascus. His chief rival among the sultan's Arab coterie was Abu al-Huda al-Sayyadi, the court astrologer.[15] Despite their battles with each other and with the Albanian faction, both 'Izzat and Abu al-Huda agreed on the sultan's Pan-Islamic policy.

Another source of Arab officeholders was the family from which the amir, or grand sharif of Mecca, was selected. Many of this family of descendants of the Prophet Muhammad lived in polite exile in Istanbul. An example is the sharif 'Ali Haydar, who was appointed to the Council of State by Abdülhamid. In 1908 he was named to the restored Senate after the military coup. He subsequently became minister of pious foundations, vice president of the Senate, and nominal amir of the Hijaz during World War I.[16]

On the whole, however, the number of Arabs who were re-

---

and the bureaucracy after 1912 and strict centralization were the chief impetus behind secessionist thinkers (C. Earnest Dawn, *From Ottomanism to Arabism* [Urbana: Univ. of Illinois Press, 1973], and Zeine N. Zeine, *The Emergence of Arab Nationalism* [Beirut: Khayat's, 1966]).

[14] For a list of Arabs prominent in the central government and court, see Muhammad Bayhum, *Kawafil al-'urubah wa ma wakabaha khilal al-'usur* (Beirut: Matba'at al-Kashf, 1948–50), II, 17.

[15] For 'Izzat Paşa see Philippe De Tarrazi, *Tarikh al-sihafat al-'arabiyyah* (Beirut: Matba'at al-Adabiyyah, 1913–33), II, 215–20. I have not been able to consult Butros Abu-Manneh's Oxford dissertation, "Some Aspects of Ottoman Rule in Syria in the Second Half of the Nineteenth Century: Reformers, Islam and Caliphate."

[16] George Stitt, *A Prince of Arabia* (London: Allen and Unwin, 1940), pp. 86–160.

cruited into the upper civil service remained low in comparison to their numbers in the empire. Representation in Parliament and in the central organization of the Committee of Union and Progress was less than the Arabs' percentage of the population.[17] In an attempt to gain support by the C.U.P., six Arabs were appointed to the Senate in 1914. The policies of the C.U.P. were even more centralizing than those of Abdülhamid, with the added feature of being oriented toward Turkish culture.

A rather larger number of Arabic speakers became military officers than top bureaucrats. Military schools had been established in Damascus in 1848 and Baghdad in 1875. Although military training remained centered in Istanbul, it was possible, especially after the 1880s, to go through the initial stages in the Arab provinces. Arab officers were assigned to Arabic-speaking military units.[18] In 1886, the only year when the information is available, it is estimated that there were 3,200 Arab officers in the Ottoman Army. Over sixty sons of local notables in the Yemen and Hijaz were commissioned in the Ottoman Army in 1890.[19]

The policies Abdülhamid adopted in his administration of Syria and the Hijaz were necessarily based on the preceding regimes' activities. The basic innovation of his reign in Syria was his attempt to gain favor with the Sunni section of the population by building new mosques and schools, making gifts to local charities, giving medals to prominent notables, and reorganizing provincial governments.[20] In the areas where Ottoman authority could not be extended immediately, he used the traditional policy of divide and rule by such stratagems as setting one Bedouin

[17] Feroz Ahmad, *The Young Turks* (Oxford: Oxford Univ. Press, 1969), p. 155; Ahmed Mohammed Harran, "Turkish-Syrian Relations in the Ottoman Constitutional Period (1908–1914)," Diss., Univ. of London, 1969, p. 159, n. 101; Davison, "Nationalism," pp. 28–30.

[18] Griffiths, "Reorganization," pp. 23–28, 80, 94, 105, 177; Shaw and Shaw, *History*, II, 86, 103.

[19] Griffiths, "Reorganization," pp. 78, 103.

[20] A. L. Tibawi, *A Modern History of Syria* (London: Macmillan, 1969), pp. 179–83; Tawfiq 'Ali Barru, *Al-'Arab wa al-Turk fi al-'ahd al-dusturi al-'uthmani, 1908–1914* (Cairo: The Arab League, Institute of Higher Arab Studies, 1960), p. 33.

tribe against another or encouraging family rivalries for office.

Ottoman control of the vilayet of Syria was assured, at least in its larger cities; the Hijaz was basically outside the jurisdiction of Ottoman officials, even in Mecca and Medina. The military, political, financial, and religious leaders of the vilayet of Syria were concentrated in Damascus, its capital. The central Ottoman government was able to determine their choice. Despite the relative lack of attention paid to Syria during the first fifteen years of Abdülhamid's reign, the vilayet witnessed the extension of effective Ottoman control into areas where it had not existed before. This was due in large part to the personal ability and long tenure of the vali, Hüseyin Nazim Paşa, whose first term as vali was between 1896 and 1908. Large landowners and Muslim urban notables were represented in advisory councils; they were able to remain the moderators between the government and its citizens.

The Syrian vilayet budgets, insofar as they are presently known, indicated that the area was on the whole a financial asset to the empire.[21] Expenditures were almost entirely on internal security: the judiciary, police, and provincial aid to imperial troops.

The Fifth Army headquarters was in Damascus. During the Russian-Ottoman War of 1877–78 over 100,000 troops, mostly reserves, were called up in Syria. Unfortunately, there is no indication how many were sent to Anatolia or Europe and how many remained in Syria. The Syrian divisions were later used extensively in the Yemen fighting. So many were sent that the Druzes in Hauran probably had the largest single armed force left in the vilayet. Troops spent weeks or even months in reaching battle areas such as the Caucasus, Yemen, and Thrace. In the event of war with a European power enjoying naval command of the Mediterranean, Syrian troops would not be able to use water transport to reach their destination. Poor transportation on land also limited Ottoman strength against Bedouins, the Druze, and any group living far from the few cities fully controlled. The movement of large numbers of troops in the desert was limited by lack of sufficient water and animals to transport them. Regular

---

[21] For the budgets for 1900–1901 and 1902–1906/7, see F.O. 195/2313, Devey (Damascus) to Lowther, 14 September 1909.

troops, even if mounted on camels, were less used to the strate-
gems and tactics desert warfare demanded than their Bedouin
opponents. Lack of mobility and particularly the expensive nature of the transport available hindered the expansion of Ottoman
authority in the area south of Damascus.

The most important factor in the economy of Syria was water.
Systematic agriculture was possible only where regular, ample
sources of water existed. Grain production in South Syria was
limited to the Hauran and the area around Irbid, Ajlun, Salt, and
Amman. South of Madaba cultivation was irregular. Since population followed agriculture, of the perhaps three million people
who lived in Syria only about 85,000 lived in the Karak Sanjak
(Karak, Salt, Maan, Tafila and their districts) and 200,000 in the
Hauran Sanjak.[22] Tribal raids and internal feuding were causes of
the relative underpopulation in addition to lack of water.

Growth in the economy was mainly in the form of horizontal
geographical expansion using the same methods of farming as
before. Increase in agricultural production depended upon obtaining easy transportation to markets in as safe, quick, and especially cheap a manner as possible. Innovations did take place
along the Mediterranean coast in the 1890s and 1900s in the raising of citrus fruits for export. Tours to Jerusalem and Damascus
became a source of revenue in the 1890s.[23] After the completion
of the Beirut-Damascus coach road in 1863, the seaport of Beirut
grew as merchandise passed in greater volume from and to the
interior. The largest city in the interior of Syria, Damascus, was
linked to the coast.[24]

Foreign economic investment was concentrated initially in the
coastal areas and Mount Lebanon. Although French interests in

[22] F.O. 195/2311, Devey (Damascus) to Lowther, 18 March 1909; Dawn,
From Ottomanism, p. 149 n. 8; Vital Cuinet, *Syrie, Liban et Palestine* (Paris: Leroux, 1896); 'Ali al-Husni, *Tarikh Suriya al-iqtisadi* (Damascus: Matba'ah Badai'
al-Funun, 1342).

[23] Al-Husni, *Tarikh*, pp. 264–65, 289.

[24] For a discussion of Damascus's economy at the turn of the twentieth century, see Dominique Chevallier, "Un exemple de résistance technique de
l'artisanat syrien," *Syria* 30 (1962), 324; idem, "A Damas, production et société
à la fin du XIXe siècle," *Annales Economies-Sociétés-Civilisation*, 19 (1964), 971.

the interior grew after 1903, the area south of the Hauran remained financially untouched by Europeans.[25] Intervention in the economy by the Ottoman central government itself was limited to occasional bans on the export of grain in time of famine.[26]

Throughout the nineteenth century the territory east of the Jordan and south of the Hauran was sparsely populated, inhabited chiefly by semisedentary and nomadic Bedouin. They were dependent for their income upon irregular agriculture, animal husbandry, and the pilgrimage. Ottoman authority among them was purely nominal. After the Russo-Ottoman War of 1876, refugees from the Caucasus founded a number of villages and the town of Amman, the ancient city of Philadelphia. They received active support from Ottoman officials. The Druzes of the Hauran extended their lands after 1860 when Lebanese Druzes immigrated to the Syrian areas.[27]

Ottoman rule in the South Syrian area was restricted to the towns and some villages. Conscription, disarmament, and land registration were not enforced.[28]

Beyond South Syria there was the province of the Hijaz, which was important to the Ottoman Empire because of the two holy cities of Mecca and Medina. The entire Muslim world sent pilgrims as well as gifts to the Hijaz. Imports of food and other items were paid for from the surplus of income from the pilgrims and by gifts from the central government and Egypt.[29]

[25] William Shorrock, *French Imperialism in the Middle East* (Madison: Univ. of Wisconsin Press, 1976), pp. 138–39.

[26] F.O. 195/2245, Devey (Damascus) to O'Conor, 12 November 1907; FRA, 328, Bompard (Constantinople) to Ministry, 6 March 1912.

[27] Baha id-Din Toukan, *A Short History of Trans-Jordan* (London: Luzac, 1945), p. 7; Frederick G. Peake, *A History of Jordan and Its Tribes* (Coral Gables, Fla.: Univ. of Miami Press, 1958), pp. 223–24; René Dussaud and Frédéric Macler, *Mission dans les régions désertiques de la Syrie Moyenne* (Paris: Imprimerie Nationale, 1903), pp. 25, 53.

[28] Antonin Jaussen, *Coutumes des Arabes au pays de Moab* (Paris: Lecoffre, 1908), pp. 120, 123; Gertrude L. Bell, "Turkish Rule East of Jordan," *Nineteenth Century*, 52 (1902), 233; Munib al-Madi and Sulayman Musa, *Tarikh al-Urdunn fi al-qarn al-ʾishrin* (Amman: N.p., 1959), pp. 29–30; ʾAbd al-ʾAziz ʾAwad, *Al-Idarat al-ʾuthmaniyyah fi wilayah Suriya, 1864–1914* (Cairo: Dar al-Maʾarif, 1969), p. 148.

[29] For a discussion of the economy of the Hijaz, see my three articles: "Ot-

Political authority in the Hijaz was shared between the amir
of Mecca and Ottoman officials. The amir was confirmed annually in his office by a decree from the sultan, which was sent
with the Syrian pilgrimage. Ottoman authority was exerted
when the amir died, for the sultan chose his successor from
among the male members of the Hashimite family. Ottoman intervention also occurred when amirs sought to gain too great an
independence of action. Amirs were deposed by order of the
sultan in 1851, 1856, and 1882.[30]

Although Ottoman garrisons were present in the Hijazi towns
of Jidda, Mecca, Medina, and Taif, they were insufficient to
keep order. The armed forces of the amir and his shifting alliances with Bedouin tribes maintained an uneasy peace. During
the pilgrimages there were many instances of robbery and mur-
der when pilgrims traveled between towns.[31] Bedouin strength
was frequently greater than that of the military guards who escorted the caravans. Therefore, subsidies were given by the Ottoman government to tribes whose territory included the pilgrimage route.

Ottoman rule of the Hijaz cost the empire's treasury greatly.
There was neither taxation nor conscription.[32] The rulers of the
empire and of Egypt gave money and supplies to the province; it
was an expense to rule the Hijaz, not a financial advantage.

Ottoman influence in the vilayet did not have to counter European or Christian traders and merchants. Christians were limited in their travel to Jidda and the immediately surrounding
area. As a result imports, exports, and credit were controlled by
Muslim banking and commercial houses.

toman Subsidies to the Hijaz, 1877–1886," *International Journal of Middle East-
ern Studies*, 6 (1975), 300–307; "The Financial Basis of Ottoman Rule in the
Hijaz, 1840–1877," in Haddad and Ochsenwald, *Nationalism*, pp. 129–49; and
"Muslim-European Conflict in the Hijaz," in press.

[30] Ismail H. Uzunçarşılı, *Mekke-i Mükerreme Emirleri* (Ankara: Türk Tarih
Kurumu Basımevi, 1972), Butros Abu-Manneh, "Sultan Abdülhamid II and
the Sharifs of Mecca (1880–1900)," *Asian and African Studies*, 9 (1973), 1–21;
and William Ochsenwald, "The Jidda Massacre of 1858," *Middle Eastern Studies*,
13 (1977), 314–26.

[31] *Al-Liwa* (Cairo), 17 October 1905; Landau, *Hejaz Railway*, p. 68.

[32] FPM, 1, Querry (Jidda) to Hanotaux, 10 August 1896.

Between 1882 and 1914 there were only three amirs of Mecca:
'Awn al-Rafiq (r. 1882–1905), 'Ali ibn 'Abd Allah (1905–8), and
Husayn (1908–16). 'Awn al-Rafiq and 'Ali overlapped with the
unusually long tenure of Ahmed Ratıb Paşa as Ottoman vali of
the Hijaz (1893–1908).[33] Ratıb Paşa and the amirs divided revenues as well as authority. A portion of the rent of camels taken
by pilgrims between Mecca and Medina went to each. Power in
the towns of Mecca and Jidda remained largely in the hands of
the amir. The amirate's income may have been about T.L. 150,
000 per year.[34] Bribery of Istanbul officials was a drain on both
the vali's and amir's incomes.

A decline in the number of pilgrims from 1896 to 1903 resulted in a decrease in the amir's revenue and the overall prosperity of the Hijaz. The low point was reached in 1899 when
only about 30,000 came to the Hijaz by sea.[35] The pilgrimage by
land was longer and more dangerous though perhaps less expensive for some pilgrims than that by sea. Although estimates of
the numbers of pilgrims going from Damascus to Medina by
land are dubious, after the opening of the Suez Canal it seems
likely that most pilgrims went to the Hijaz by sea. The round-
trip land route took about four months (including stays in Mecca
and Medina), at a cost of about T.L. 50 per pilgrim. The cost of
sending the symbols of Ottoman sovereignty to the Hijaz with
the land pilgrimage and the money paid to the tribes to ensure
safe passage were borne by the central and provincial government. Unlike the income from the pilgrimage, these costs were
fairly steady. In the early 1900s the central government paid T.L.
35,000 and the vilayets of Beirut and Syria about T.L. 100,000.[36]
The leader of the Syrian caravan in this period was a prominent

[33] Sulayman Musa, *Al-Husayn ibn 'Ali wa al-thawrat al-'arabiyyat al-kubra*
(Amman: Dar al-Nashr, 1957), pp. 14–15; F.O. 195/2126, Devey (Jidda) to
O'Conor, 14 October 1902.

[34] F.O. 195/2286, Monahan (Jidda) to Constantinople, 8 May 1908; Ibrahim
Rif'at Paşa, *Mirat al-haramayn* (Cairo: Matba'ah Dar al-Kutub al-Misriyyah,
1344/1925–26), II, 126.

[35] FPM, 3, Lepissier (Jidda) to Constantinople, 25 January 1911.

[36] Al-Marawani, *Al-Khatt*, p. 2; Karl Auler, *Die Hedschasbahn* (Gotha: J.
Perthes, 1906), pp. 23–24; René Tresse, *Le pèlerinage syrien aux villes saintes de
l'Islam* (Paris: Chaumette, 1937), p. 295; Landau, *Hejaz Railway*, pp. 49–50;
F.O. 195/2144, Richards (Damascus) to O'Conor, 10 February 1903; F.O. 195/
2190, Richards (Damascus) to Townley, 10 January 1905.

Damascus notable who was appointed by the Ottoman central government.

Once the pilgrimage left Damascus it was nearly autonomous. The reasons were the same as those that led to the autonomy of the Hijaz Province: the distance from Istanbul was great, transport and communications were slow, and the challenges posed by the tribes demanded immediate solutions.

Transportation and Centralization in Syria and the Hijaz

The weakness of the Ottoman Empire in South Syria and the Hijaz was recognized by Sultan Abdülhamid. His program for overcoming this problem was the construction of the Baghdad Railroad to Aleppo and then building an Ottoman-controlled railroad network to connect Syria with the Hijaz.[37]

Although the role of railroads in increasing military capacity, and therefore political centralization, was obvious by 1900, railroad building in the Ottoman Empire had also had several negative results. These were the increase of foreign economic control over the state and the separation of the empire into economic spheres of influence along the tracks of the railroads controlled by different European companies.

Ottoman efforts to have their own railways had been frustrating failures. The Haydarpaşa-Izmit Railroad, built by a French company, was operated by the Ottoman government for less than two years. It was then leased to a concessionaire but ultimately was sold to an English firm.[38] Other Ottoman attempts at their own railroad operations included the Mudanya-Bursa Railroad and the Bellova-Uskub line, which were victims of the Ottoman bankruptcy of 1875, and, in the case of the latter, the Peace of Berlin.[39] From that time on, all railroads in the Ottoman

[37] Centralization through railroad construction played a major role in Abdülhamid's plans in all of the empire. By 1907–8 total trackage had been tripled to 5,883 kilometers (Shaw and Shaw, *History*, II, 227).

[38] George Young, comp., *Corps de droit Ottoman* (Oxford: Clarendon Press, 1905), IV, 117–18.

[39] J. Courau, *La Locomotive en Turquie d'Asie* (Brussels: Guyot, 1895), p. 4; Young, *Corps*, IV, 62 n. 1, 70–71.

Empire were privately owned and controlled by foreign concessionaires.

In 1880 the minister of public works wrote a memorandum
that determined government railroad policy for nearly twenty
years. He felt that the empire's need for railroads could be met
only by European capitalists. Government construction and operation were too expensive and inefficient, he claimed, especially
since the empire did not have any surplus funds for capital in-
vestments.[40]

Since profits were doubtful on many of the privately owned
railroad lines, the companies usually received guarantees that
they would have a minimum income per kilometer of track built
and in operation. The kilometric guarantees helped secure both
the construction of lines that were economically precarious and
the permanent presence of foreign financial interests. Frequently
revenues for the guarantees were assigned to the Ottoman Public
Debt Administration for collection. Between 1896 and 1906 the
Ottoman central government and the O.P.D.A. paid foreign
railroad companies at least T.L. 700,000 per year.[41]

The advantages and disadvantages of foreign railroads could
be seen in Syria. By 1900 a number of lines had been built or
planned by foreign capitalists. In the north the German-domi-
nated Baghdad Railroad was to pass near Aleppo on its way to
Iraq. The central area of Syria was served by a French-owned
company, the Damas, Hama et Prolongements (D.H.P.), which
ran from Beirut to Damascus and then south to Muzeirib. In
Southern Syria the Jaffa-Jerusalem Railway was also controlled
by French capitalists, but was isolated from the D.H.P. A British company began construction of a Haifa-Damascus Railroad,
although no more than a short stretch of track was ever actually
built.

In addition to the problems of foreign control and kilometric
guarantees, these railroads were isolated from one another, dif-

---

[40] Gabriel Charmes, *L'avenir de la Turquie* (Paris: Calman-Levy, 1883), pp.
211–13.

[41] Based on statistics found in Alexis Rey, *Statistique des principaux résultats de
l'exploitation des chemins de fer de l'Empire Ottoman* (Constantinople: N.p.,
1896–1913) for the years indicated in the text.

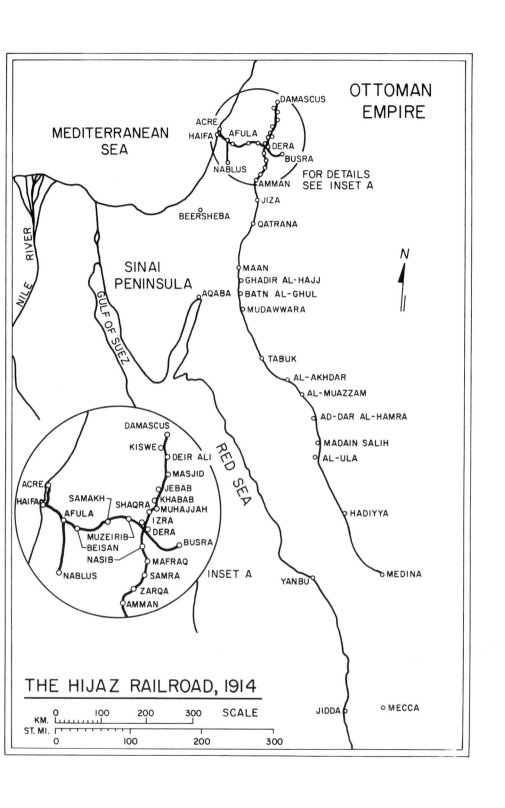

MEDITERRANEAN SEA

OTTOMAN EMPIRE

DAMASCUS
ACRE
HAIFA
AFULA
NABLUS
DERA
BUSRA
AMMAN
JIZA

FOR DETAILS
SEE INSET A

BEERSHEBA
QATRANA

SINAI PENINSULA

NILE RIVER

GULF OF SUEZ

AQABA

MAAN
GHADIR AL-HAJJ
BATN AL-GHUL
MUDAWWARA

TABUK
AL-AKHDAR
AL-MUAZZAM
AD-DAR AL-HAMRA
MADAIN SALIH
AL-ULA

N

RED SEA

DAMASCUS
KISWE
DEIR ALI
MASJID
JEBAB
ACRE
HAIFA
SAMAKH
SHAQRA
KHABAB
MUHAJJAH
AFULA
IZRA
DERA
MUZEIRIB
BEISAN
NASIB
BUSRA
NABLUS
MAFRAQ
SAMRA
ZARQA
AMMAN

INSET A

HADIYYA

MEDINA

YANBU

THE HIJAZ RAILROAD, 1914

KM.
ST. MI.

0   100   200   300   SCALE

0   100   200   300

JIDDA   MECCA

fered in the gauge of their tracks and thus could not use the same equipment, and in the case of the D.H.P. had to cross the Lebanon and Anti-Lebanon Mountains, thereby adding to the expense of freight shipment. The lines ran from Mediterranean ports inland. They were not linked in the interior or on the coast. During the 1900s part of the problem was solved when the D.H.P. secured concessions for railroads linking Riyaq on the Beirut-Damascus line to the Homs-Hama-Aleppo line. Homs was also linked to the Mediterranean at Tripoli (Lebanon). With the financial collapse of the British Haifa-Damascus Railroad the northern part of Palestine was left out of this growing network.[42]

None of the companies considered the construction of railroads that would go far south of Damascus. With the exception of the area covered by the short D.H.P. branch to Muzeirib, the likelihood of sufficient freight and passengers to create profits in that region was too small. Yet the sultan felt that a railroad there was necessary for military and political purposes.

The project was not completely new. As early as 1864 a proposal had been made to the Ottoman government for a railroad linking Damascus and the Red Sea.[43] In 1874 an Ottoman army officer had suggested that a railroad to Medina-Mecca was necessary to secure Ottoman control in the Hijaz. In the late 1890s Muhammad Insha Allah began a propaganda campaign in Indian and Arab newspapers for the creation of a railroad passing through the holy cities and ending in Yemen. The Ottoman Council of Ministers discussed the idea of a railroad to the Hijaz in August 1898.[44]

[42] For the history of the D.H.P. see Eleftériadès, *Les chemins de fer*; the Jaffa-Jerusalem Railroad is discussed briefly in Cuinet, *Syrie*, pp. 606–9. A brief résumé of the activities of the Syrian-Ottoman Railroad Company (British) between 1890 and 1899 is in F.O. 78/5186, O'Conor (Constantinople) to Salisbury, 1 August 1899.

[43] The originator of the idea was Ferdinand Zimpel, an American civil engineer, who also made plans for a Jaffa-Jerusalem Railroad (Hermann Guthe, "Die Hedschasbahn von Damaskus nach Medina," *Länder und Volker der Türkei* 7 [1917], 3; Frank G. Carpenter, *The Holy Land and Syria* [Garden City, N.Y.: Doubleday, Pope and Co., 1922], p. 26; Landau, *Hejaz Railway*, p. 8).

[44] Muhammad Insha Allah, *The History of the Hamidia Hedja Railway Project* (Lahore: Central Printing Works, n.d.), pp. 1–15, 26.

Construction of a telegraph line to the Hijaz began while discussions on the railroad project proceeded. The telegraph served as a test of the efficacy of the plans for the railroad. Matériel, personnel, and financing were exclusively Ottoman. Under the direction of Sadiq Paşa al-Muayyad, a member of a prominent Damascus family and an aide-de-camp of the sultan, construction was rapid and cheap. Donations of money and wood for telegraph posts were solicited. Ottoman soldiers performed most of the labor. Construction was stopped at Medina because the Bedouin tribes living between Medina and Mecca opposed the telegraph, probably at the instigation of the amir.[45]

In 1900 Sultan Abdülhamid decided to order the construction of a railroad between Damascus and Mecca. It would be financed, built, and operated by the Ottoman Empire alone. In this project he hoped to promote his dual goals of increasing the empire's capacity and autonomy. He said that a railroad to the Hijaz would allow him to defend the area more readily from possible foreign attacks;[46] at the same time, since it had the character of a holy railroad and would serve pilgrims on their way to Mecca, it would increase his reputation for piety and his claim to be the caliph of all Muslims. This railroad was, then, to be the single physical embodiment of the Pan-Islamic movement. If the empire could handle the project using only Ottoman sources of supply and personnel, it would indicate to Europeans and Ottomans alike that technical and economic independence was possible. Other large-scale public works in the future might be constructed by Ottomans alone.

On 2 May 1900 the sultan announced that a railroad would be built. He appealed to the Muslims of the empire and the world to support it. Construction of the Hamidiye Hijaz Railroad was to begin on 1 September 1900, the twenty-fifth anniversary of Abdülhamid's accession to the throne.

---

[45] FRA, 319, Savoye (Damascus) to Delcassé, 1 May 1902.
[46] Ali Vahbi Bey, *Avant la débacle*, p. 122.

The Syrian pilgrimage path, near Tabuk

The descent at Batn al-Ghul

A wadi near Maan

Chapter II

Construction

THE CONSTRUCTION OF a railroad was one of the most complex administrative and engineering tasks undertaken by government in the nineteenth century. For even the most efficient of organizations this presented a considerable challenge. For a non-European government there was also the problem of adopting foreign technology and methods.

In addition to the technical difficulties of building a long railroad line, the contradiction inherent in the Ottoman goals of autarchy and efficiency appeared in every stage of construction of the Hijaz Railroad. An Ottoman state railroad presented an opportunity to avoid foreign dependence as well as a means of achieving the long-range goals of increased military, technological, and financial strength. Sultan Abdülhamid II and his advisers attempted to use only Ottoman citizens and Ottoman goods for construction. When this goal was put into practice, the equally strong desire to complete the railroad quickly and inexpensively could not be achieved. The result of the conflict between efficiency and dependence upon foreigners was a victory for rapid construction as the chief goal, with supervision of the construction by foreigners as the best means of achieving it.

The Creation of a Local Administration

The creation of an Ottoman staff to supervise the construction of the Hijaz Railroad was a unique act. Almost all Ottoman railroads and utilities had been built and managed by foreign or only nominally· Ottoman companies. The Ottomans expected failure because they lacked personnel experienced in railroad work; this expectation was in itself a barrier to success. Skeptics pointed to what Westerners considered inefficient and corrupt practices of the Ottoman government in its political administration and argued that similar behavior was inevitable in railroad construction that was dominated by Ottoman officials. Ottoman administration in the Arab provinces frequently suffered from sluggishness, unwillingness to assume responsibility, divided authority, and a lack of knowledge of the Arabic-speaking subject peoples.

Many of these problems did not occur in the construction of the Hijaz Railroad because with a few exceptions money was made available on a regular basis; the sultan's desire for rapid completion of the line was a constant prod, spurring on officials who were slow to act; and supervision of construction was entrusted to one body, the Damascus Central Commission, and eventually to one man, the head engineer, Meissner Paşa.

The Istanbul Central Commission of the Hijaz Railroad restricted itself to the supervision of donations, purchasing supplies abroad, and overall financial accountability. All other matters were delegated to the Damascus organization or kept in the hands of the sultan and his second secretary, 'Izzat Paşa. Work in Damascus was done by special committees that reported to the local commission. Although theoretically the decisions of such a committee would have to be cleared by both the Damascus and Istanbul authorities and then go to the sultan, 'Izzat in fact frequently by-passed these channels in the interest of securing rapid communications and speedy action.[1]

---

[1] FRA, 321, Péan (Damascus) to Delcassé, 16 February 1904.

Membership in the Damascus Central Commission was kept small. Its original members, who were appointed by the sultan, represented the chief sources of power in the vilayet of Syria. Nazim Paşa, the vali of Syria since 1896, remained as chairman until his removal from the vilayet in 1908. The presence of the head of Syria's civil authority assured close cooperation between the provincial government and the construction. Adib Nazmi, secretary of the Damascus City Council and editor of *Suriya*, the official vilayet journal, was the secretary of the commission.[2] 'Abd al-Rahman Paşa Yusuf, the leader of the Syrian pilgrimage to Mecca, by his membership gave to the railroad not only the benefit of his experience with the country to be crossed but also the approval of the chief Ottoman figure associated with the land pilgrimage. His strong support of the railroad lessened possible opposition to it based on religious conservatism.[3] Muhammad Fawzi Paşa al-'Azm, a member of one of the most influential families in Damascus, represented the notables of the city; he was also on the administrative council of the vilayet of Syria.

While information on the operations of the Damascus Central Commission is almost totally lacking, it seems that the commission's two chief functions were the channeling of money from Istanbul to the contractors and workers and overall supervision and coordination of the various governmental and railroad committees that dealt with construction. The commission was successful in achieving the first function, since there was little reported mismanagement of money. The multitude of new committees was brought together through the central commission.[4]

The Haifa branch line presented particularly great problems

---

[2] *HDL*, pp. 1–2; *TF*, 3 Nisan 1905, p. 6.

[3] 'Abd al-Rahman Paşa Yusuf (1874?–1920) was a member of a wealthy Kurdish landowning family long settled in Damascus and closely related to two former leaders of the pilgrimage. He was the son-in-law of Muhammad Fawzi al-'Azm. 'Abd al-Rahman's Ottoman civil rank of bala, obtained in 1908, was second in Syria only to the vali, who was a vezir.

[4] FRA, 321, Péan (Damascus) to Delcassé, 16 February 1904; H. Slemman, "Où en est le chemin de fer La Mecque," *Revue de l'Orient Chrétien*, 6 (1901), 148.

of coordination because most of it lay outside the vilayet of Syria. Beirut Vilayet officials constituted a local directing committee in Beirut for the Haifa branch similar to the one in Damascus. Members included the vali of Beirut; the kaimakam of Haifa; and representatives of the Vakıf, Engineering, Parks and Forests, and Accounting departments of the vilayet government. In addition to keeping separate financial records, the Beirut committee helped supply the construction workers with clothes and animals. Most of its authority was eventually assumed either by Damascus or by Hamdi Paşa, the former vali of Basra, who was director of construction for the Haifa line, 1902–6.[5]

Inspection of the construction was carried out by the vali of Syria or other members of the Damascus commission, as well as by at least one foreigner, Otto von Kapp, who reported to the Istanbul commission.[6]

Von Kapp's report of 1905 suggested that the changes made in the administration between 1900 and 1905 resulted in rapid improvement in the speed and efficiency of construction. Initially there had been many organizational and technical failures.

In 1900 construction was supervised by Ottoman Army officers. Their chief was Mehmed Ali Paşa, formerly chief of staff of the Second Division (Istanbul). His small staff consisted of six Ottoman engineers who were sent to Damascus in June 1900. Only two of them had had any prior experience with railroads; they had been inspectors of foreign-owned railroads in Anatolia. An Italian, La Bella, was hired as chief engineer. He arrived in Syria only in November 1900.[7]

The initial surveys for the track were entrusted to 'Ali Rida al-Rikabi, then on the staff of the Fifth Army (Damascus), and to Mukhtar Bey, an Ottoman Army engineer who joined the pilgrimage in 1900 in order to obtain a rough plan of the route used

[5] *TF*, 30 Adhar 1902, p. 4; 19 K al-Th 1903, p. 4; 22 Haziran 1903, pp. 4–5; 24 Ab 1903, p. 5.

[6] A progress report on Hijaz Railroad construction is in the archives of the India Office: see IO. Von Kapp, a German engineer, was inspector for the Hama-Aleppo section of the D.H.P.

[7] F.O. 195/2075, Richards (Damascus) to O'Conor, 15 June 1900; Rambert, *Notes*, p. 107.

by the camel caravans to Mecca.[8] Most of these first steps, taken while the central government's attention was on fund raising, turned out to be failures. Mehmed Ali Paşa was court-martialed for maltreatment of the soldiers working on the line, especially for not providing them with sufficient food. The engineers working with the construction crews mutinied at Muzeirib, the railhead, because of lack of pay. Several fled to Egypt after being court-martialed in Damascus. The surveys south of Muzeirib were so badly done that thirty kilometers in the first section had to be redone. In the first six months of construction only twenty kilometers of earthwork were prepared for railroad tracks. The foreign chief engineer was dismissed at the end of his year's contract.[9] Only Mukhtar's route survey and his proposed route for the railroad were adopted from the first period of Ottoman control of construction.

The sultan demanded more rapid construction. Hasan Paşa, chairman of the Istanbul Central Commission, ordered the vali of Syria to send a telegram every day about the progress made in construction.[10] The sultan and 'Izzat Paşa repeatedly sent messages to the Damascus commission asking for the details of construction. This pressure ended the first phase of attempts at construction and resulted in the decision to create a new administration with a new division of responsibilities. Most importantly, new and more experienced personnel were to be hired.

Ottoman control over the technical aspects of construction was abandoned in the interest of greater efficiency. However, large questions of policy continued to be decided in Istanbul, and local command was retained in Ottoman hands. An Ottoman general was appointed coordinator of construction and placed on the Damascus Central Commission. Perhaps because this officer, Kazim Paşa, had had experience with Western military technology, he was willing to allow the foreign engineers

[8] *TF*, 30 Nisan 1900, p. 4. Al-Rikabi later became governor of Medina (1910) and subsequently a leader in the Arab nationalist Kingdom of Syria after World War I.

[9] F.O. 195/2097, Richards (Damascus) to O'Conor, 3 December 1900, 7 January 1901, and 26 January 1901; Slemman, "Où en est," p. 146.

[10] *TF*, 10 K al-A 1900, p. 4.

who came to dominate construction the leeway they demanded. At the same time his high status, military experience, willingness to cooperate with Europeans, and strong drive for action made him a perfect agent for the sultan. Kazim remained as general director of the Hijaz Railroad until he was appointed vali of the Hijaz in 1908.[11]

Kazim's control over construction was frequently only approval of the decisions taken by Heinrich Meissner. Meissner was a German railroad engineer, trained in Dresden and Vienna, and a veteran of several railroads built by foreign companies in the Ottoman Empire. He spoke Ottoman, English, and Italian as well as German.[12] More important than his technical and linguistic qualifications was his realistic and friendly attitude toward working with Ottoman officials and technicians. He believed in the possibility of reforming the empire; in view of the antipathy and scorn for the Ottomans felt by many foreigners, this was unusual. Meissner was willing to delegate responsibility to his Ottoman subordinates.[13]

Through personal tact and experience with Ottoman administration, Meissner Paşa was able to avoid interference by Kazim and the Damascus Central Commission. There were few time-consuming conflicts. He was decisively overruled only once, in 1904, when he opposed moving construction headquarters to Dera. Some disagreements with Kazim over the scope of his control were settled when Meissner secured a two-year contract in which he was guaranteed more freedom from supervision and exemption from criticism.[14]

Meissner was aware of the limitations of Ottoman workers.

---

[11] Müşir Kazim Paşa, an opponent of Sultan Abdülhamid in the 1890s, had been vali of Shkodër and commander of a division stationed in Istanbul. His appointment to Syria was viewed as a polite and honored exile from the capital. In 1902 he was the highest-paid Ottoman officer in all of Syria (F.O. 195/2122, Richards [Damascus] to O'Conor, 13 March 1902).

[12] Herbert Pönicke, "Heinrich August Meissner-Pascha und der Bau der Hedschas- und Bagdadbahn," *Welt als Geschichte*, 16 (1956), 197.

[13] Durham, "The Hedjaz Railway," Cairo Military Intelligence (1907), p. 8.

[14] F.O. 195/2165, Richards (Damascus) to O'Conor, 7 March 1904; F.O. 78/5451, Richards (Damascus) to O'Conor, 15 January 1903.

An example is his recommendation that, wherever feasible, bridges be built of stone, not iron, in order to permit easier repairs by an Ottoman railroad repair crew that would not be familiar with iron bridges.[15]

For his successful administration of construction, Meissner was rewarded in several ways. He was given freedom to recruit engineers of his own choice, including many who had worked with him for the French-owned Régie Générale des Chemins de Fer. He was honored by the sultan: he received the title of paşa, a number of awards, and a higher salary. In the last years of his contract he received a base salary of about T.L. 1,000 plus T.L. 2 for every kilometer of track completed. Only when the main line was completed in 1909 did he leave the Hijaz Railroad for work on the Baghdad Railroad. During 1915 he came back to Syria and supervised the Hijaz Railroad's extension toward the Suez Canal.[16]

Working relationships between Ottoman officials and foreign engineers were not always so smooth as that of Meissner and Kazim. The first two chief engineers under Hamdi on the Haifa branch resigned. Construction supervision was transferred to Meissner, who could get along with Hamdi.[17]

The replacement of the initial heads of construction by Meissner and Kazim was followed by appointments of a number of new, better-qualified men at all levels. Sadiq Paşa al-Muayyad al-'Azm, a military attaché of the sultan and a Damascus notable, became Kazim's chief assistant in 1902. Sadiq had been in charge of the building of the Hijaz telegraph line from Syria to Medina. He was familiar with the geography of the area and the problems involved in large-scale activity in the desert. In 1903 he was appointed to the Damascus Central Commission.[18]

[15] F.O. 78/5451, F. Maunsell, "Report on Syrian Railways, 1905," p. 9.

[16] FRA, 321, Péan (Damascus) to Delcassé, 16 February 1904; *TF*, 11 Aylul 1905, p. 4; Turkey, Başbakanlık Arşivi, Bab-ı Ali Evrak Odası, 271327, Report by military officers to the Grand Vezir.

[17] FRA, 321, Gaillardot (Haifa) to Delcassé, 14 November 1904; *TF*, 19 T al-A 1903, p. 4.

[18] *TF*, 16 T al-Th 1903, p. 4; 30 T al-Th 1903, p. 6.

Mukhtar Bey, one of the original surveyors, became Meissner's chief deputy. He was a graduate of the Engineering School
of Istanbul. By 1904 he had become chief inspector of the main
line; he was also in charge of the construction of the Yarmuk
Valley bridges. Subsequently Mukhtar, from his base at Medina,
supervised the building of the line by the local garrison.[19]

The chief sources of recruitment of Ottoman bureaucrats and
upper level engineers for the Hijaz Railroad were the Ottoman
Army and Navy. Eight officers from the Fifth Army composed
the first construction staff for the Haifa branch. The Mediterranean squadron of the fleet provided a number of officers who
helped in transporting goods to the railhead, inspecting completed work, and supervising locomotives and other machinery.[20]

The Recruitment of Personnel

The struggle over the use of Ottoman or foreign personnel in the
administration occurred in all sections of construction. Criteria
of efficiency, technical knowledge, and experience overcame the
original desire to use only Ottomans for engineers, foremen, and
construction crews. A mixture of Ottoman military and private
Ottoman contractors with foreigners took place. The degree to
which the mixture was military or civilian depended upon the
technical problems encountered in construction, the ability of
Meissner to retain Christian employees, the growing experience
of Ottoman citizens at all levels of the railroad, and the relative
cost and success found in using the different groups.

When Meissner took control of the Hijaz Railroad, he had to
create an engineering staff. Though he drew largely on Germans, the engineering staff included other Europeans. An example is the Haifa branch, which in 1904 employed four Germans and two Belgians as engineers. About forty engineers were

[19] Eleftériadès, *Les chemins de fer*, p. 169; *TF*, 27 Haziran 1904, p. 3; Auler,
Die Hedschasbahn, I, 27.

[20] *TF*, 4 Adhar 1901; 21 Nisan 1902, p. 4; 4 Nawwar 1903, p. 4; 11 Tammuz
1904, p. 6.

employed between 1903–7; on the average one-half were foreigners, and most of these were Germans.[21]

Foreign engineers were limited in their usefulness by their inability to understand the language of the people with whom they worked. They were unable to go close to Medina because they were Christians. An even more serious liability was the resentment by Ottoman Army officers of them simply because they were not Ottomans. Three European section chiefs in supervisory positions as well as others in lower jobs quit because of maltreatment by Ottoman officers.[22]

Gradually more Ottoman engineers were hired. Meissner had originally objected to graduates of the Ottoman-controlled Istanbul Engineering School on the grounds that they lacked practical experience. This argument was somewhat circular since the chief reason there were so few graduates with work experience was the use of foreign engineers by foreign-owned railroads. Sultan Abdülhamid forced the use of many graduates from the Engineering School upon Meissner by ordering one-half of each graduating class to work for the Hijaz Railroad. Although in 1903 there were only seven men recruited in this fashion, the number increased after 1905.[23]

Although little detailed information is available about the Ottomans who worked for the Hijaz Railroad, engineers employed in the early years of construction seem to have had some training in Europe.[24] As a result, they were presumably familiar with not only Western techniques but also Western languages. One example is Nazif Bey al-Khalidi (1875–1916), a member of a prominent Jerusalem Sunni Muslim family. He graduated from both Istanbul University and the Ecole Polytechnique in Paris. Dur-

[21] F.O. 195/2165, J. Monahan (Haifa) in Drummond-Hay (Beirut) to O'Conor, 28 January 1904; Guthe, "Die Hedschasbahn," p. 16.

[22] F.O. 195/2144, Richards (Damascus) to O'Conor, 23 March 1903.

[23] *MKA-SAH I*, p. 971; *TF*, 23 Shubat 1903, p. 2; 28 K al-A 1903, p. 4.

[24] Marcel Castiau, "En Syrie: le long du chemin des pèlerins de la Mecque," *Bulletin de la Société Royale de Géographie d'Anvers*, 27 (1903), 33–34, 47; A. Goodrich-Freer, *In a Syrian Saddle* (London: Methuen, 1905), p. 108; W. Tyler Bliss, "The Sultan's Dummy Railway," *Harper's Weekly*, 50 (1906), 734.

ing his four years with the Hijaz Railroad immediately following his return from France, he was in charge of the construction of the railroad station in Damascus, a number of bridges, and some tunnels. He also worked with the construction in the Amman area.[25]

Ottoman soldiers were used for common labor; they were especially useful in moving earth for the embankments upon which the rails were placed. This was the chief job demanding large amounts of unskilled labor. Foreign laborers, skilled and unskilled, were used occasionally for earthmoving, but generally they were employed in aspects of construction that demanded special training or experience.

When building its lines in Northern Syria, the Damas, Hama et Prolongements Railroad had used 1,500 foreign workmen out of about 5,000 workers employed.[26] Similarly, the Hijaz Railroad employed at least 600 foreign workmen, including Italians, Greeks, and Montenegrins. They were mostly used for building bridges, some culverts, tunnels, and other stonework. Their employment posed many problems. South of al-Akhdar (km. 760 from Damascus) there were no Christians; Egyptian Muslims were employed to replace them. In 1903 French, Italian, and Arabic were used by the workers while many of the foremen were German speakers. The religious and linguistic differences caused clashes between workers and local officials. Foreign workers were accused of brawling, drinking excessively, and being immoral. The Construction Administration tried to do away with some of these difficulties by suggesting that foreign workmen take provisional Ottoman citizenship so as to avoid constant recourse to diplomatic intervention for settling violent episodes. The European consuls rejected the idea.[27]

---

[25] Interview with Mrs. Ahmad Tuqan in Amman, 18 January 1970. Mrs. Tuqan is the daughter of Nazif al-Khalidi.

[26] *TF*, 6 K al-Th 1902, p. 5.

[27] Goodrich-Freer, *In a Syrian Saddle*, pp. 73, 100; F.O. 78/5452, Richards (Damascus) to O'Conor, 8 February 1902; Muhammad al-Batanuni, *Al-Riḥlat al-Hijaziyyah li . . . ʾAbbas Hilmi Basha . . .* , 2d ed. (Cairo: Matbaʾat al-Jamaliyyah, 1329/1911), p. 234; F.O. 195/2122, Richards (Damascus) to O'Conor, 5 April 1902. The young Mustafa Kemal (Atatürk) visited the workers' cafe in

Ottoman soldiers provided a large pool of untrained and cheap manpower, accustomed to working together and living under discipline. Starting with the arrival of two companies (about 600 men) in Beirut in June 1900, the number of soldiers increased rapidly. By 1901–2 there were nearly 5,700. Of these, 3,000 were infantry from the Fifth Army; 2,400 were in two railroad battalions; 200 were members of army engineering units; and fifty were in the telegraphy unit of the Fifth Army.[28] Some troops were sent from the Jebel ed-Druze and Hauran areas in Syria to work on the railroad. This movement of garrisons from a frequently rebellious region emphasizes the urgency felt by military commanders under orders from Istanbul for rapid construction. Illness, desertion, and losses caused by soldiers reaching the end of their military duty reduced effective strength. As a result about 2,000 men from the Sixth Army (Baghdad) were sent to join the work force in 1906. While 7,500 men were working on the main line by 1907, 1,800 from the Medina garrison began construction from Medina north toward the advancing troops.[29]

Communication inside the army detachments was complicated by language barriers. The nature of communications within the multilingual Ottoman Army is still largely unknown, but it is likely that most of the soldiers of the Fifth and Sixth armies spoke only Arabic. Although some officers were Arabs, many were Turks whose knowledge of Arabic was limited. Noncommissioned officers and heads of construction gangs were selected for their ability to understand both languages.[30]

Ottoman civilians were employed by contractors who undertook to build stations and bridges and do other work. They were used especially on the Haifa line's Yarmuk Valley section, where

---

Damascus (Lord Kinross, *Ataturk* [New York: Charles Scribner's Sons, 1964], pp. 23–30).

[28] *TF*, 11 Haziran 1900, p. 5; Auler, *Die Hedschasbahn*, p. 26.

[29] F.O. 78/5452, F. Maunsell (Constantinople) to O'Conor, December 1902; F.O. 371/154, Surtees (Constantinople) to O'Conor, 30 August 1906; Pönicke, "Meissner-Pascha," p. 199; F.O. 371/350, F. Maunsell to Gleichen, 16 April 1907.

[30] Durham, "The Hedjaz Railway," p. 4.

military labor had proved to be too slow. The delays there resulted in the placing of bids to contractors for construction of
sections of the line. About one-sixth of the total work force in
1904 was civilian workers employed by contractors.[31]

When contractors tried to hire workers, they encountered the
suspicion that work on the railroad was really corvée and would
not be paid. It is true that in some cases peasants were given the
option of working for the railroad in return for not paying the
corvée road tax. Forced labor was exacted from some Palestin-
ians who had not paid taxes.[32]

The capacity of the Ottoman goverment to provide skilled mechanics and others familiar with railroad construction from
among its own employees was small because the potential pool
of trained manpower was small. Nevertheless, there was an attempt to provide trained workmen when available.

A long tradition of technical training was utilized when the
Istanbul Imperial Arsenal was asked for men to help in the transfer of supplies at Haifa to the branch line.[33]Army telegraphers
who had worked with the Hijaz telegraph line helped construct
the railroad's own telegraphic system. They were also used as
engine drivers as were some naval mechanics. Army sappers performed a multitude of tasks: they were locomotive operators,
workshop assistants, locksmiths, and carpenters. In order to
have Muslims available who could handle construction in the
Hijaz, the Construction Administration hired Christian artisans
for training purposes. Italian stonemasons taught one and one-
half companies of troops how to build small station buildings
and culverts.[34] With increasing frequency Ottoman soldiers performed more complex tasks on the main line.

[31] *MKA-SAH I*, pp. 971–72; F.O. 78/5451, F. Maunsell, "Report on the
Syrian Railways, 1905," p. 10.

[32] *TF*, 17 K al-A 1900; FRA, 320, Gaillardot (Haifa) to Delcassé, 26 April
1903; F.O. 195/2140, Drummond-Hay (Beirut) to O'Conor, 14 April 1903.

[33] *TF*, 1 Tammuz 1907, p. 4.

[34] *TF*, 10 Shubat 1902, p. 4; 9 Tammuz 1906, p. 5; Tresse, *Le pèlerinage*, p.
324; M. Hecker, "Die Eisenbahnen der asiatischen Türkei," *Archiv für Eisenbahnwesen*, 27 (1914), 1315; F.O. 371/156, Auler Pasha, "Report," p. 6; Durham, "Hedjaz Railway," p. 2, 36; F.O. 371/350, F. Maunsell, "Report on the
Hedjaz Railway, 1907," pp. 2, 36.

The Conditions of Work

The conditions under which soldiers and civilians worked may have influenced their efficiency as much as their previous training. Again, Ottoman efforts were marked by initial failure followed by improvement caused at least partially by following Europeans' advice.

The major problems for workers resulted from the weather and absence from families. Health problems developed from the extreme variations between heat and cold, lack of water, and especially recurring attacks of communicable diseases. Attacks of scurvy and dysentery were followed by typhoid and in 1902–3 a devastating attack of cholera. Between Dera and Amman at least four hundred workers died from cholera; many fled the area. Health conditions for workers were improved only in 1907 when doctors and pharmacists were sent from the Fifth Army and several hospitals were opened. Separation from wives and families involved all but a few engineers and administrators who were able to afford housing accommodation near the railhead.[35]

Perhaps the chief attraction of working on the Hijaz Railroad for Ottoman soldiers was a reduction in the time they had to spend in active service. Three years with the railroad counted as four years' service elsewhere. After two years on the railroad officers could obtain special promotions.[36] Promises of rewards for service in difficult areas were not unusual. Their being carried out in practice was a precondition to securing the cooperation of the soldiers employed in the work. Soldiers were dismissed on time, with full travel allotments, and back pay. Promotions of officers were frequent.[37]

Another way in which the Ottomans encouraged rapid completion of the line was to offer incentive pay based on a piece-

[35] FRA, 220, Régie Générale des Chemins de Fer to D.H.P., 5 January 1903; Peake, *History of Jordan*, p. 96; Paul Fesch, *Constantinople aux derniers jours d'Abdul-hamid* (Paris: Marcel Rivière, 1907), p. 503; *MKA-SAH I*, p. 980; *TF*, 11 Shubat 1907, p. 4; personal interview with Mrs. Ahmad Tuqan, 18 January 1970.

[36] F.O. 78/5452, Richards (Damascus) to O'Conor, 13 January 1902.

[37] *TF*, 5 Aylul 1904, p. 5.

work system. Originally both civilian and military workers received a flat sum for every day worked. One of the major innovations started in 1901–2 was a series of increases in pay both to officers and men. Those not working at the railhead were awarded fixed bonuses. A captain in the army made only T.L. 4 per month; his bonus ranged from T.L. 6 to 10. A worker who made 3 to 4 Ottoman kuruş per day might receive a bonus of 19 kuruş per month. Troops engaged in earthmoving at the railhead were paid one kuruş for every cubic meter of earth moved and three for stone. They continued to receive their regular army pay. Specialists among the soldiers were paid double this rate; Italians working on cuts or tunnels received 2½ kuruş for every cubic meter of earth and 12 to 14 for rock. All who worked south of Maan had a special bonus.[38]

The rate of pay was usually of little importance to those working for the Ottoman government because of the inability of its bureaucracy to pay wages regularly, honestly, and promptly. In the case of the Hijaz Railroad, although the basic pay of the soldiers came from the War Department, the extra bonuses came from the railroad's own funds. Workers were paid in public, by hand, and in cash. High officials of the Damascus Central Commission would frequently accompany the paymasters to ensure fair treatment of the soldiers. Despite this, on at least two occasions in 1902 and 1906 there were periods when the soldiers were not paid. In 1906 a strike was averted only by Kazim's promise to satisfy the grievances of the workers.[39]

Other benefits were offered to attract workers and to improve efficiency. Imams were provided by the Ministry of Religious Foundations. In 1907 on the opening of the Tabuk-al-Ula section of the main line, 2,500 Ottoman medals were distributed to

[38] *MKA-SAH I*, pp. 971–72; *TF*, 28 K al-A 1903, p. 4; F.O. 195/2165, Young to Drummond-Hay, 23 March 1904; Guthe, "Die Hedschasbahn," p. 18; F.O. 371/350, F. Maunsell, "Report, 1907," p. 3.

[39] F.O. 195/2122, Monahan (Damascus) to O'Conor, 8 October 1902; I.O. 3288, Loiso (Mersina) to O'Conor; *TF*, 3 Haziran 1907, p. 7; R. Bidwell, ed., *Correspondence respecting the Affairs of Arabia, 1905–1906* (London: Cass, 1971), O'Conor (Constantinople) to Grey, "Report on the Hedjaz Railroad," 12 June 1906.

workers and others. Workers were given free transportation on the railroad. If they died while employed, a small sum was paid to relatives. Workers were hired with no questions asked about their backgrounds: one political opponent of Abdülhamid was hired by the railroad when he reached Syria in his flight from arrest in Anatolia.[40]

Ottoman and Foreign Contractors

Ottoman citizens and foreign nationals who were contractors for the Hijaz Railroad illustrated two seemingly contradictory aspects of construction. Although by contemporary European standards the contractors were small and inefficient, in practice they managed to finish the jobs they were given more economically and quickly than the Ottoman Army. At the same time, the use of Ottoman contractors meant that foreigners and foreign intervention could be avoided.

Meissner initially described the contractors he encountered as being incapable and unreliable, especially in fulfilling financial agreements. Since they were small firms they lacked large sums of capital. Unable to wait for payment until the completion of construction, the contractors had to ask for advances from the railroad. Compounding the contractors' difficulties, the railroad occasionally paid them late. Profits were supposed to be between 10 and 12 percent. If it became necessary for them to borrow large sums for capital expenses, the contractors were unable to make a profit. The small profit margin was a strong incentive for inflating the cost of construction in bids submitted to the government.[41]

Most of the work done by contractors was on the Haifa branch. All of the Jordan-Dera section was let to contractors.

---

[40] *TF*, 25 Haziran 1900, p. 4; 2 Aylul 1907, p. 4; 14 K al-Th 1907, p. 4; Sulayman Musa, *Suwar min al-butulah* (Amman: Al-Matba'at al-Hashimiyyah, 1968), p. 123.

[41] F.O. 195/2097, Richards (Damascus) to O'Conor, 11 December 1901; F.O. 195/2122, Monahan (Damascus) to O'Conor, 8 October 1902; F.O. 195/2041, Abela (Haifa) to Drummond-Hay, 12 May 1903; FRA, 321, Péan (Damascus) to Delcassé, 16 February 1904.

They also undertook to build some bridges and stations on the
main line. Later, following the completion of the main line, the
need for speed on the Afula--Nablus branch in Palestine induced
the railroad to hire contractors to build thirty-seven kilometers
of track.[42]

The same problems associated with the use of foreign administrators, engineers, and workers existed for contractors. The
Hijaz Railroad sought to use Ottomans to the maximum but
found itself at times compelled to employ Europeans resident in
Syria.

In order to establish some government control over contractors, the terms governing bids issued in 1901 began with a state-
ment that only those who were Ottomans or who knew local
conditions and the local labor market could apply. Contractors
could not subcontract without permission from the railroad. Inspectors could reject matériel not meeting the specifications.
Losses to the railroad caused by nonfulfillment would be met
from guarantees paid by the contractors. If, after completion and
final inspection, the railroad rejected the work done by the con-
tractor, appeal could be made only to the chief engineer, Meissner, and then to the vali of Syria.[43] This was an attempt to block
the intervention of foreign consuls on behalf of individual foreign
contractors. The degree to which the specifications in the bids
allowed the Ottoman government in practice to control the contractors is unknown.

The parts of the line that were let to bidders were divided
between Ottoman and foreign contractors. For example, on the
sixty-eight kilometers of the Haifa branch east of the Jordan
River the following division was made: two German contractors
received two sections; an Italian had two; an Austrian had one;
and Damascenes gained three.[44] On the other hand, stonework

[42] F.O. 195/2165, Richards (Damascus) to O'Conor, 25 May 1904; *TF*, 28 T
al-A 1901, p. 4; Peter Dieckmann, "Die Zweiglinie Affula-Jerusalem," *Zeitschrift des Deutscher Palästina-Vereins*, 37 (1914), 269.

[43] *TF*, 7 K al-Th 1901, pp. 7–8.

[44] F.O. 78/5451, Drummond-Hay (Beirut) to O'Conor, 7 June 1904. For a
slightly different account see FRA, 322, Gaillardot (Haifa) to Delcassé, 14
November 1904.

on the main line seems to have been awarded mostly to Ottomans.

The only two Ottoman contractors about whom biographical information is available were Dr. Husayn Haydar Bey and Sa'd al-Din al-Dimashqi. Haydar Bey's ability to compete with Europeans for contracts may have been related to his background. He was a member of a notable Mutawali family of Baalbek and a nonpracticing physician. He built the section from Muazzam (km. 822) to ad-Dar al-Hamra (km. 880) as well as stations south of ad-Dar al-Hamra, including the Medina Station. At least some European stonemasons were employed by him. Sa'd al-Din built stations in the Kiswe-Maan area and undertook some stonework. He wrote an account of an inspection tour he made in 1904 in which he complained of the lack of trains used to bring supplies to the workers. Sa'd was a critic of the D.H.P. Railroad.[45]

Construction Matériel

Obtaining the matériel used for construction of the Hijaz Railroad was in itself a considerable task. Ordering and transporting the large quantity of goods taxed the abilities of all sections of the Construction Administration. At first the Istanbul authorities tried to obtain matériel inexpensively by using only Ottoman sources, but these were unable to meet the needs of the railroad; recourse to European producers became necessary for most items.

The single most expensive category in the cost of construction matériel was the supply of rolling stock and rails from Europe. In 1900 the Istanbul Central Commission ordered that rails and some other equipment be made at the imperial shipyards and Naval Arsenal in Istanbul. The railroad cars were to be made at the arsenal; only six locomotives were to be bought in Europe. Wooden crossties were supposed to be cut at no expense to the railroad by workers in the imperial forests. The War Ministry offered to manufacture out of its own resources five kilometers

---

[45] Al-Marawani, *Al-Khatt*, pp. 27, 50; Durham, "Hedjaz Railway"; *TF*, 18 Nisan 1904, p. 3; 8 Aylul 1902, p. 5; 27 Haziran 1904, pp. 2–3.

of rails per day. Provincial governments were ordered to send metal to the Istanbul Arsenal for melting down and refashioning into rails.[46]

Nearly all these attempts at self-sufficiency in matériel failed. The reason for the attempt to make the railroad's supplies was probably that the sultan's servants were eager to try something, even though futile, to show their master that action was underway. As early as June 1900 an investigation ws begun to see whether buying rails in Europe would be cheaper than making them in Istanbul. In addition to cost it became clear that the Naval Arsenal could prepare at most 250 meters of rail per day. Only a few rails, some first-class passenger cars, and a mosque car were made at the arsenal.[47] Although most of the wooden crossties came from imperial forests in Anatolia and Syria, they were cut and shaped by contractors using private labor. Almost all of the manufactured matériel used in construction came from Europe and the United States, and a preponderant share was from Germany and Belgium.[48]

European purchases were handled in Istanbul by the Central Commission; its expenditures by the end of Abdülhamid's reign amounted to T.L. 1,403,805. After the Revolution of 1908 it was accused of accepting bribes and being wasteful. Zihni Paşa, minister of public works during the latter years of Abdülhamid, defended its honesty and efficiency. According to Zihni, the committee inspected European goods and then wrote handbooks for bidders that set up strict criteria for the purchase of rails, crossties, and rolling stock. It sent negotiators to Europe to establish the groundwork for bids. Prices were estimated by the builders on the basis of costs in Western Europe plus transportation expenses. Next, comments from Damascus and Haifa were solic-

[46] *TF*, 21 Nawwar 1900, p. 5; 28 Nawwar 1900, p. 4; 4 Haziran 1900, p. 5; "Sikkah hadid al-Hijaz," *Al-Muqtataf*, 25 (1900), 95; Tresse, *Le pèlerinage*, p. 309.

[47] *TF*, 25 Haziran 1900, p. 4; H. Slemman, "Le chemin de fer de Damas–La Mecque," *Revue de l'Orient Chrétien*, 5 (1900), 519; "Khatt al-hadid al-hijazi," *Al-Manar*, 3 (1900), 283–85; *TF*, 1 Ab 1904, p. 4.

[48] Charles M. Pepper, *Report on Trade Conditions in Asiatic Turkey* (Washington, D.C.: Government Printing Office, 1907), pp. 9, 14.

ited concerning prices and quality. Only after approval by the
Damascus Central Commission and the Imperial Treasury were
contracts signed. On at least one occasion these safeguards resulted in the rejection of defective goods and switching orders
away from their manufacturer. In the case of the only purchasing
committee that was sent to Europe whose membership is
known, there were Ottoman officials who were capable of supervising European manufacturers. It included a major who worked
in the Imperial Arsenal, engineers from the Ministry of Public
Works, and Admiralty officials familiar with steel manufacturing.[49]

Construction Problems

In addition to the problems presented in setting up an organization, securing a labor force, and buying the goods needed for
construction, a number of challenges to the capacity of the empire to build the railroad became apparent only while the construction was underway.

The first of these was the absence of water or, occasionally,
the presence of too much of it. Some storage tanks built by the
Abbasids and early Ottomans still existed in the desert areas
along the pilgrimage route below Maan. The railroad's need for
water was unfortunately more extensive than the pilgrimage facilities could meet. Besides providing for the 5,000 or so men
working on the line, water was needed for mixing with lime and
for the operation of steam locomotives. At first camels were
hired from Damascus contractors to bring water; then the railroad bought cast-iron water tanks and mounted them on
flatbeds. Old wells were repaired and new ones dug. There remained large distances between the wells which had no water:
al-Akhdar (km. 860) to Madain Salih (km. 955), Maan (km. 459)
to Mudawwara (km. 572), and others. Construction crews and
the men who later operated the line had to depend upon shipments of water arriving by train.[50]

[49] Zihni Paşa, *Beyan-i hakikat* (Istanbul: Ahmet Ihsan, 1327/1909), pp.
35–36; *HDL*, pp. 11–12; *TF*, 29 Tammuz 1901, p. 4; Slemman, "Où en est,"
p. 147.

[50] Guthe, "Die Hedschasbahn," pp. 23–24; F.O. 371/156, Auler, p. 16.

In both the relatively better-watered area north of Maan and
in the desert south to Medina there were a large number of wadis
which, though usually dry, were filled after a rain. These required culverts and bridges built in such a way that the water
could pass without destroying the embankment. The danger of
floods was particularly great because soldiers filled in some wadis
with earth and placed tracks on top as a temporary measure so
that the railhead could be advanced even though the stonemasons who built the permanent bridges were far behind. Floods
in the Yarmuk Valley caused delays in construction in 1904 and
1906. About 950 bridges were eventually built on the entire
line.[51]

Most of the long bridges that posed special engineering problems were in the Yarmuk and Jordan valleys. From Haifa to Dera
there were six iron bridges, four of 110 meters and two of fifty
meters. There were also six tunnels whose length ranged between forty and 170 meters.[52]

Variations in temperature were extreme. For example, in the
winter at Tabuk the temperature was as low as $-5°C/21°F$. The
temperature in the summer in Jordan has reached $55°C/131°F$.[53]
Hard physical work in such temperatures must have been very
difficult.

Topography presented fewer problems than did the climate.
Most of the track was built on flat or slightly rolling terrain. It
was estimated that the tracks covered 210 kilometers of plains,
154 of steep hills, and 1,164 of slightly hilly areas.[54]

The route of the main line was close to, and sometimes exactly
corresponded with, the path used by the Damascus-Medina pilgrims. The Haifa branch was more uneven. From sea level at
Haifa the line ascended to eighty meters along the Plain of Marj
Ibn Amir (Esdraelon) in a distance of forty kilometers, then de-

[51] *TF*, 25 K al-Th 1904, p. 7; Hecker, "Die Eisenbahnwesen," p. 1066; al-
Marawani, *Al-Khatt*, p. 26.

[52] Al-Marawani, *Al-Khatt*, p. 31.

[53] Al-Batanuni, *Al-Rihlat*, p. 314; "Die Hedschasbahn," *Archiv für Eisenbahnwesen*, 39 (1916), 298.

[54] Hecker, "Die Eisenbahnwesen," p. 773; al-Marawani, *Al-Khatt*, pp.
11–17, describes the topography of the railroad.

scended to 246 meters below sea level along the Jordan; in only forty kilometers it went from that level to 376 meters on the Jordanian hills and then to the plain around Dera at 530 meters. Two river valleys—the Jordan and Yarmuk—had to be traversed in a line only 168 kilometers long.[55]

The Hijaz Railroad was built in as simple a manner as possible. With the exception of the excessive allowance of length for curves, it corresponded to contemporary European railroad construction.[56]No technical difficulties were found in such areas as the depth of the ballast, the steepness of gradients, and the like. The chief reason so few technical problems existed was the decision to use narrow-gage track.

Wide-gage track of 1.45 meters was standard over most of the Ottoman Empire, but not in Syria. By 1914 only the French system north of Riyaq and the Baghdad Railroad were wide gage; all the rest of the lines were narrow gage of 1.05 meters. The advantages of narrow-gage track included considerably less expense for rails and all of the rolling stock needed for operations, since everything was smaller. Costs for matériel were perhaps one-half what a wide-gage line would have entailed. Another advantage was that the D.H.P. narrow-gage railroad to Muzeirib could be used to transport engines and cars to the Hijaz system. Technical assets were an increased ability to handle steep ascents and less need for length in curves. The chief disadvantage was that the top speed on narrow gage was about half that possible on wide gage. Carrying capacity was also less. The use of narrow gage was an admission that the railroad's freight and passenger traffic would be small in quantity compared to that handled by lines using wide gage.

Branches

As the line reached south of Damascus its distance from Beirut became greater. Goods from outside Syria arrived at that harbor and were sent by the D.H.P. to Damascus and Muzeirib. By

[55] Eleftériadès, *Les chemins de fer*, p. 173; al-Marawani, *Al-Khatt*, p. 31.
[56] Int. Res., pp. 14–24.

October 1901 about 346,000 tons had been sent to Beirut.[57] A bottleneck soon developed: the D.H.P. could not increase its carrying capacity over the mountains between Damascus and Beirut. After several palliative measures were tried, it was decided that a branch from the Mediterranean inland to the main line must be built.

The first step in meeting the supply problem was to assign naval personnel to help move goods from the ships in Beirut harbor to the quays and then from the port to the D.H.P. Railroad terminal. The Beirut Vilayet urged the D.H.P. to construct a short rail link between the port and its main station in Beirut. Because of recurring financial crises the D.H.P. delayed this project, which it also desired. It was finally opened in March 1903.[58]

The D.H.P. and the Hijaz Railroad in May 1900 agreed to reduce by 45 percent the cost of shipment for construction matériel. Rebates to large shippers were customary with the D.H.P. The Hijaz Railroad was expected to spend about T.L. 300,000 at the standard rate of charges in the planned ten-year period of construction. Estimated costs of shipment with the reduction included were put at about T.L. 16,000 for 1903. In the midst of negotiations for the purchase of the Damascus-Muzeirib line, the D.H.P. denounced the earlier reduction.[59] This step was an additional reason for the sultan's decision to proceed in 1903–4 with the building of a branch line from Haifa to Dera. It would provide competition for the Beirut-Damascus line of the D.H.P. since it would serve the same grain-exporting regions of Syria and the import business of Damascus. A Haifa-Dera line would also transport construction matériel needed for the Hijaz Railroad's main line at no expense to the Ottoman government other than its original construction cost.

The planned British Haifa-Damascus Railroad was bought in 1902. Ottoman construction of the branch line began in April

---

[57] F.O. 195/2097, Richards (Damascus) to O'Conor, 5 October 1901.

[58] *TF*, 8 T al-A 1900, p. 5; Eleftériadès, *Les chemins de fer*, p. 61.

[59] F.O. 195/2075, Drummond-Hay (Beirut) to De Bunsen, 26 September 1900; FRA, 321, Péan (Damascus) to Delcassé, 16 February 1904; FRA, 321, Savoye (Damascus) to Delcassé, 1 September 1903.

1903 as a lever to put pressure on the D.H.P. during negotiations. Serious operations commenced only in late 1903. The formal opening of the line was in September 1905. Some trains used in construction went inland following this, but commercial traffic started on a regular basis only in June 1906.[60] When opened, the Haifa branch line cut 125 kilometers from the Beirut-Damascus-Dera trip on the D.H.P.

Dera (km. 123), the terminus of the Mediterranean branch of the Hijaz Railroad, was nearly 1,200 kilometers away from Medina. The need for another branch closer to Medina was clear. Because of the suspected opposition of the amir, building the part of the railroad planned to run from Jidda to Mecca and then north seemed impracticable. From the beginning of the extension of Ottoman control to South Syria in the 1890s, troops had been sent from Damascus to Maan and then on to Aqaba, where they embarked on ships for Yemen. Since the number of harbors on the Red Sea was small, Aqaba was a natural site for the terminus of another branch of the railroad.

Unfortunately, the harbor at Aqaba itself proved not to be adequate for unloading large ships. Nearby, close to the Egyptian-garrisoned small fort of Taba, a safe anchorage existed at Firaun Island. Both Taba and Firaun were, according to the Egyptians and the British, part of Sinai and therefore under Egyptian control. When the Ottoman Empire tried to expand its control over Taba, the whole question of Egypt's relationship to the empire was raised.

It is outside the scope of this work to evaluate the international ramifications of the Taba incident. The military results of the Hijaz Railroad for Egypt and Ottoman use of a branch line during the war to attack the Suez Canal are discussed in chapter 5. In the period before 1905 a condition of mutual anxiety concerning Sinai had slowly arisen in Cairo and Istanbul. The settlement of 1840 between the Ottomans and the Egyptians had been reconfirmed at the accession of every new ruler of Egypt. In 1892 the decree investing 'Abbas II as khedive had raised questions concerning the frontier of Sinai that were settled in favor

---

[60] Guthe, "Die Hedschasbahn," p. 20.

of the status quo. Egyptian garrisons were voluntarily withdrawn afterward from the camps where Egyptian pilgrims had
rested during their trips to the Hijaz. Although Egyptian troops
left the Hijaz, the British extended police and military activities
in Sinai. They feared Ottoman expansionism as a danger to the
Suez Canal. For them the Ottoman political control then coming
into existence in South Syria was a possible threat to the canal.[61]

During early 1905 the Ottoman government appointed a
mayor for Aqaba, improved its harbor somewhat, and finished
a telegraph line to the village. In December the Istanbul Central
Commission decided to build a Maan-Aqaba branch. On 15 February 1906 Ottoman troops crossed what the British considered
to be the frontier and occupied Taba. Their claims on territory
extended considerably beyond Taba and Firaun.[62]

England sent troops to reinforce the Egyptian garrison. The
British Mediterranean fleet moved to Piraeus, where it threat-
ened Istanbul. An ultimatum to the sultan was grudgingly ac-
cepted by the Ottomans; they withdrew their troops from Sinai
on 11 May 1906.[63] The location of the Sinai frontier was settled
according to the British position. As a result, the Ottomans concluded that a branch line from Aqaba inland to the Hijaz Railroad would not be possible.

A number of other branch lines were, however, added to the
Damascus-Medina and Haifa-Dera system before 1914. In 1906
a four-kilometer extension from just outside Damascus to the
heart of the city was decided upon after it became clear that a
station in the inner city would gain new freight and passengers
for the railroad. A complex of storage and repair facilities was
established around the Damascus stations.

Another short line built in 1911–13 was the Haifa-Acre
branch of eighteen kilometers; it linked the two towns together

[61] Victor Bérard, "L'incident de Tabah," *Revue de Paris*, 13 (1906), 218–23;
idem, *Le sultan, l'Islam et les puissances* (Paris: Colin, 1907), pp. 171–78; F.O. 78/
5452, Richards (Damascus) to O'Conor, 18 March 1905.

[62] *TF*, 29 Nawwar 1905, p. 1; 19 Haziran 1905, pp. 4–5; FRA, 323, Boppé
(Constantinople) to Rouvier, 11 December 1905; René Pinon, *L'Europe et
l'Empire Ottoman* (Paris: Perrin, 1909), pp. 372–6.

[63] Bérard, *Le sultan*, pp. 60, 178; Pinon, *L'Europe*, pp. 394–95.

around their common bay. The motives for building the thirty-nine kilometer extension from Dera to Busra were both commercial and military. Busra was in the heart of the Hauran, where a great deal of wheat was grown; it was also close to the Jebel ed-Druze, one of the chief centers of Druze anti-Ottoman rebellions. The ability to move troops to the area had been important in Sami Bey al-Faruqi's military operations against the Druze in 1909–10. Transportation of troops was much easier after the building of a railroad that reached at least halfway into the center of rebellion.

Military communications inside Palestine and south toward Gaza and El-Arish were important both for defense of Palestine from the British navy and as potential support for an Ottoman overland attack on the Suez Canal. The Ottomans built a line toward Beersheba in the period before World War I. From Afula on, the Haifa-Dera line tracks were completed in February 1913 to Jenin (km. 17). By the time of Ottoman entry into the war, the railroad had reached Sabastiya and was close to Nablus. The announced Ottoman goal before the war was to link Jerusalem with the Hijaz system and thereby provide a link with the hitherto isolated Jaffa-Jerusalem Railway.

By the end of 1914 the Hijaz Railroad had 1,585 kilometers of track in operation.[64] The main line had been extended to reach areas of military and commercial importance fairly close to it. The major addition, the branch in Palestine from Haifa to Dera, when extended south toward Jerusalem and beyond toward Egypt, would add all of the strategically important areas of Palestine to the Hijaz Railroad network.

The Rate and Cost of Construction

The most important criteria in judging the efficiency of the Ottoman Empire's construction of the Hijaz Railroad are the speed with which it was built, the quality of the work done, and the cost of building the line.

---

[64] [Hijaz Railroad] *Hicaz Demiryolunun Varidat ve Masarif-i ve Terakki-i Inşaatı* . . . , 1330 (Istanbul: Evkaf-i Islamiye Matbaası, 1334/1915–16), p. 3.

The speed of construction can be seen by examining the completion of the various sections of the line. After the completion of the field survey by the army, the Ottoman military administration began construction from the end of the D.H.P. tracks at Muzeirib southeast toward Dera. This section of approximately fifteen kilometers was completed only in September 1901. Reasons for slowness were numerous: the most important was the necessity of the new administration under Kazim and Meissner to redo much of the initial work. Nearly as important was the time necessary to get any large organization into operation. Establishing an organization, obtaining materials from foreign manufacturers, hiring contractors, raising money—all needed time before functioning at full efficiency. A third reason for slowness at the beginning was the low productivity of soldiers and officers who received only army pay. Meissner's incentive payments resulted in an immediate increase in productivity. Instead of the one-third cubic meter of earth moved per day per soldier, starting in early 1901 a soldier moved on the average one and one-fourth cubic meters.[65]

During 1901 preparatory work was done beyond Dera. The opening of the constructed sections on 1 September 1902 took place in Zarqa, only eighty kilometers south of Dera. In the two and one-half years since Abdülhamid had called for the building of the railroad, less than 100 kilometers had been finished: at that rate it would have taken thirty years to reach Medina.

Over the next six years the Construction Administration was able to increase the rate of construction. It was able to do so chiefly because of support received from Istanbul and the administration's overcoming of the initial delays.

The sultan backed the project in every way possible. His personal support impressed upon all officials the necessity of success in the construction. After 1902 money was no problem. Equipment flooded into Beirut, and after the completion of the Haifa branch transport of supplies to the main line was rapid. Meissner obtained more workers and more soldiers. The men working on the line became familiar with the techniques of railroad construc-

[65] F.O. 195/2097, Richards (Damascus) to O'Conor, 8 March 1901.

tion. Soldiers were drafted to the railroad and taught technical skills. Others already possessing special talents were sent to the railroad from elsewhere in the empire.

A whole series of technical and environmental problems was overcome once Meissner assumed control. After mid-1901 base camps were supplied water by railroad cars. Decisions did not have to go all the way back to Damascus after the establishment of a base camp in Maan in 1904. During 1903–4 contractors started to function more efficiently. Instead of temporary tracks over wadis, more permanent bridges and short culverts were built by contractors, foreign stonemasons, and, increasingly, by Ottoman soldiers. For example, in addition to the kilometers built in 1903 there should be added about 600 bridges and culverts, some wells, and eleven stations.[66] Eventually ninety-six stations were built.

Nearly 250 kilometers of track were opened on the sultan's accession anniversary in September 1903. After the hope of buying the D.H.P.'s Damascus-Muzeirib track had to be given up, a parallel line was built from Damascus to Dera (124 kilometers), and Zarqa-Qatrana (123 kilometers) was added to the already built Muzeirib-Dera-Zarqa line.

Ali Bey, commander of the troops working at Qatrana and south of there, estimated that, given adequate supplies, his troops could put down a maximum of four kilometers of rails per day. The actual rate varied between one and three kilometers per work day; the embankment went more slowly than the rails.[67]

In the period 1904 to early 1906 construction on the main line was slowed by diversion of effort to the Haifa branch. In 1904 and 1905 only 247 kilometers were added to the Damascus-Medina track. This was nearly the same amount as had been built in 1903 alone.

With the opening of the Mudawwara-Tabuk (120 kilometers) section on 1 September 1906, only slightly more than half of the

[66] *TF*, 18 Nisan 1904, pp. 2–3; Hecker, "Die Eisenbahnen," p. 1313; Angus Hamilton, *Problems of the Middle East* (London: Nash, 1909), p. 282.

[67] *TF*, 27 Haziran 1904, p. 3; *Al-Ahram* (Cairo), 1 July 1904, p. 1; *MKA-SAH I*, p. 972.

1,300 kilometers between Damascus and Medina had been traversed. Including the Haifa branch, construction between September 1902 and September 1906 had averaged about 186 kilometers per year. On the other hand, the difficulty of construction
in the Yarmuk Valley would not be encountered again. The phe-
nomenal burst of speed in 1907 and 1908 was therefore a continuation of the last three years with fewer natural and organizational problems to hinder the construction workers. The 610-
kilometer distance between Tabuk and Medina was completed in
August 1908, and the opening ceremony held on 1 September
1908 at Medina.

Though the line was said to be open, much of the railroad was
incomplete. Immediately after the opening ceremony the construction effort turned to providing stations, marshaling yards,
repair facilities, commercial storehouses, and permanent bridges.

Evaluation of the quality of the work has been favorable. Perhaps the best witness to the quality of the construction has been
the operation of parts of the line without major repair from 1908
to the present. An American firm surveying the line for repairs
in the 1950s said that "the civil engineering design of the existing
line proves to be well conceived and executed, considering the
methods in general use at that time."[68]

Construction of the Hijaz Railroad was faster, without sacri-
ficing quality, than privately built Ottoman railroads. Though
different geographical and financial factors make direct comparison difficult, the 183 kilometers built per year from September
1900, to September 1908 were more by about one-third than
other railroads in the empire averaged in their construction.[69]

The cost of the railroad was less than similar lines elsewhere
in the Ottoman Empire. 'Izzat Paşa estimated in 1900 that the
cost per kilometer would be T.L. 2,000—about half of what he
thought private construction of the railroad would entail.[70] By
1904 only about T.L. 1,500–1,700 was being spent on construction; the Hijaz Railroad was one of the least expensive railroads

[68] Int. Res., pp. 6 and 22.
[69] F.O. 371/156, Auler, "Report," p. 19.
[70] *TF*, 15 T al-A 1900, p. 4.

ever built. However, the Haifa-Dera branch cost about T.L. 560,000 or about T.L. 3,450 per kilometer. This was double the average of the main track.

The total cost of construction of all branches and the main line to the end of the Ottoman fiscal year 1327 (March 1912) was T.L. 3,250,000, or about T.L. 2,120 per kilometer. If the cost of rolling stock is added, the cost was T.L. 4,283,000, or about T.L. 2,800 per kilometer. This compared favorably with T.L. 7,440 for the broad-gauge Anatolian Railroad; T.L. 7,000 for the broad-gauge Riyaq-Hama section of the D.H.P.; and T.L. 4,780 for the narrow gauge Jaffa-Jerusalem Railway. The amount invested in the Hijaz Railroad by the Ottoman government was about 11 percent of the total capital invested in privately owned Ottoman railways. The Hijaz Railroad constituted 28 percent of the total length of railroad track built in the empire outside of Egypt.[71]

The speed, efficiency of construction, and low cost of the railroad were largely the result of the forced labor of soldiers in the Ottoman Army. The success of the railroad also resulted from the free hand eventually given to Meissner and his largely European staff. After initial attempts at using Ottoman resources of personnel and equipment, the decision was made to turn to Europe for both supplies and men. Although ultimate control was retained by Ottoman administrators, most administrative decisions were made by Europeans.

Even though it was impossible to keep control of construction in the hands of the Ottomans, in marked contrast to other economic institutions, foreign governmental intervention was kept to a minimum. Only the Taba incident provided leverage for foreign interference. The construction of the Hijaz Railroad demonstrated that Ottoman public works could be built only by accepting technological and organizational guidance from Europeans.

[71] My calculations based on Hecker, "Die Eisenbahnwesen," pp. 1084, 1315, 1321; Zihni, *Beyan*, pp. 31–33; "Die Hedschasbahn," pp. 289–93.

Macadamizing the bedway

Terracing, with Nazif al-Khalidi in the center

Removal of rocks

Terracing near Tabuk

Soldiers working on the track

Laying of the track by soldiers of the 2d battalion

Bridge near Amman

Bridge near Amman

Chapter III

Financing

CONSTRUCTION OF THE Hijaz Railroad was dependent upon find-
ing new sources of revenue. The total cost of the railroad was
over T.L. 4,000,000; this was about 15 percent of the Ottoman
Empire's budgeted expenditures in 1909.[1] To obtain such an
amount was especially difficult because Ottoman financial resources were already committed to other projects. Borrowing for
the Baghdad Railway, repayment of previous debts, and the expenses of the army left the state nearly bankrupt every year.
When bureaucrats and soldiers received their salaries irregularly,
it seemed impossible that a large new financial obligation could
be satisfied.

The finances of the Ottoman Empire are of importance to the
history of the Hijaz Railroad; however, the taxation policy of the
empire in itself is outside the scope of this work. The two-thirds
of the railroad's income that was not gained from donations will
be examined only briefly, for it was the campaign for donations

[1] *HD*, pp. 4–21; Feis, *Europe*, pp. 315–16 and 335–36.

that was unique. It was closely tied to the nature of the railroad and its importance to the empire. The Hijaz Railroad was presented to the Ottoman people as a work of religious charity. It was dedicated to improving the pilgrimage and to the protection and economic betterment of the Holy Cities of Islam. The religious aspect of the railroad was used as an argument in favor of its being built and operated by the empire rather than by a foreign-controlled private company. Only Muslims should construct a railroad to Mecca and Medina. If the railroad project was to be completely Muslim, then its financing must also come from Muslim sources.

There were three groups of Muslims who were the sources of funds: Ottomans who were forced to provide money for the railroad; Ottomans who donated voluntarily; and Muslims who lived outside the empire. Appeals to these groups based on religious solidarity were made by fund raisers, Pan-Islamic newspapers, and Ottoman diplomats. Gifts were collected starting in 1900.

An examination of the contribution drive between 1900 and 1908 serves to illustrate two phenomena: (1) the level of support and enthusiasm for the Hijaz Railroad and (2) the complex of emotions and ideas which centered around the idea that the Ottoman sultan-caliph was the defender of Islam. The Hijaz Railroad was a concrete expression of the Pan-Islamic movement.

Popular support for the railroad is difficult to gauge accurately because of the lack of sufficient data on donations. Although the circumstances surrounding some gifts are recorded, generalizations about donors cannot yet be made with certainty. Detailed lists from the railroad itself have been found only for an eleven-month period in 1902–3.[2] Describing Ottoman donations as either voluntary or forced is also a problem because of the reluctance of both donors and collectors to admit coercion. Yet the evidence that has been pieced together from contemporary sources indicates that most Ottoman donations were forced. Popular support for the railroad was greater outside the empire. Campaigns for contributions took place in most Muslim lands.

[2] BBA-Defter.

Available evidence indicates that the largest collections were made in Egypt and India. The total of all voluntary contributions is unknown, but it was surely far less than the total of all so-called gifts—T.L. 1,100,000.

The importance of the contribution of even small sums of money was great when seen in the context of the economic life of the Ottoman Empire. Although the price and wage structure of the empire around 1900 is largely unknown, the sacrifice gifts represented can be seen by an examination of some salaries and wages. A day laborer in Syria might have a cash income of T.L. 10 per year; a skilled workman's income could reach T.L. 20 or 30 per year. Skilled foreign workmen earned annually a maximum of T.L. 60. An Ottoman Army captain's yearly salary was about T.L. 50. The upper ranks of the Ottoman bureaucracy earned more. A brigadier general in 1907 was paid T.L. 600 per year.[3] A donation even of T.L. 10 was large by comparison to the income of most workers in the society.

The meaning the donors attached to the railroad can be judged by the amount contributed; the degree to which the contributions were voluntary; and, where such information exists, the socioeconomic level of the persons who gave money.

Financial Administration

Before contributions could begin, a central financial administration had to be created. Ottoman efficiency and honesty at the center of the collection effort spurred provincial officials to begin collecting money for the railroad in a similar manner.

In April 1900 the Hijaz Railroad project was placed under a Central Commission that met in Istanbul. The finances of the railroad were supervised by a number of agencies as well as the Central Commission. The Ministry of Public Works, the Agricultural Bank, and the Treasury participated in the financial organization. After the Revolution of 1908 the railroad's accounts came under the control of first the Prime Ministry, then the Ministry of Pious Foundations, and finally the Ministry of War.[4]

[3] *MKA-SAH I*, pp. 971–72; *TF*, 28 K al-A 1903, p. 4; 18 Shubat 1907, p. 4.
[4] *HD*, pp. 1–2; *HDL*, pp. 1–4.

A central collection committee was initially appointed by the minister of the treasury. Its chairman was a former official in the Ottoman Post Office. The functions of the committee were restricted to record keeping and the manufacture of certificates and medallions to give to donors. Certificates were printed in several denominations so that even a donor who gave a small amount would obtain a token that the donation had been received. Such certificates could be displayed as symbols of piety. The committee realized that donors outside the empire would not be able to read Ottoman so they printed certificates in several languages. Medals were made for large donors. The type of medals given to donors depended upon the amount of the gift. Three classes existed: T.L. 5 to 50, 50 to 100, and over 100.[5]

The central collection committee delegated most of the work of collection to provincial committees. Although it is known that local groups were established in most of the empire's political subdivisions, the way they functioned and their membership are largely unknown.[6] Even in matters determined by the central collection committee, such as the way donations were to be forwarded to Istanbul, the performance of the committees varied. For example, money was sent directly to the Treasury by local officials in the Beirut area. According to orders from the central collection committee, accumulated funds of more than T.L. 50 were to be sent to special groups in the capital of each vilayet for safekeeping before being sent to Istanbul.[7]

The local provincial groups, insofar as their composition can be ascertained, seemed to be composed of the chiefs of the Ottoman government in the area. With little outside supervision they had the opportunity of committing embezzlements from the Hijaz Railroad funds. Only two cases of outright tampering with railroad money were detected. The first involved Mehmed Zihni Efendi, the kaimakam of İncesu in Anatolia, who was re-

[5] Muhammad Kurd ʾAli, *Kitab khitat al-Sham* (Damascus: Al-Matbaʾat al-Taraqqi, 1925–1928), III, 188; *TF*, 25 Haziran 1900, p. 4; 1 T al-A 1900, p. 6; 29 Nisan 1901, p. 5.

[6] BBA-Defter lists more than twenty vilayets.

[7] F.O. 78/5452, O'Conor (Constantinople) to Salisbury, 27 July 1900; *TF*, 20 Ab 1900, p. 5; 11 Shubat 1901, p. 4.

moved from his post. Murshid Efendi of the accounting department of Hama misappropriated T.L. 400 of railroad funds, was found guilty, and punished.[8]

Official Donations

The first gift to the Hijaz Railroad was made by the sultan. Abdülhamid's donation was soon followed by presents from the members of his court. He had given the equivalent of one month of his civil list. This set an example for other top officials. The need to equal the sultan's donations spread from the top of the court to all parts of the Ottoman government. The grand vezir gave T.L. 810–this was one month's salary.[9] Hasan Paşa, minister of the navy and chairman of the Central Committee of the railroad, gave T.L. 1,500. Zihni Paşa, the minister of public works; the chief of naval operations; the head inspector of the army; and 'Izzat Paşa al-'Abid—all contributed substantial sums.

Feeling pressure to imitate the ministers, whole departments pledged contributions. The Istanbul employees of the Treasury promised T.L. 1,580. Muslim employees of the Tobacco Régie pledged one month's salary, as did the English workers in the Imperial Naval Yards in Istanbul. The officials of the Ottoman state steamship company made a similar pledge. Between July 1902 and June 1903 the Ottoman Army contributed T.L. 8,532. Some gifts were made in kind. The Ereğli coal mines gave 458 tons of coal. Another gift was the 7,000 wooden crossties sent by the people of Menteşe.[10]

Some provincial bureaucrats are also known to have made donations. The vali of Beirut contributed T.L. 100. The deputy governor and the vilayet's treasurer each gave T.L. 25. Many

[8] *TF*, 18 Shubat 1901, p. 4; 3 Haziran 1901, p. 4; 16 T al-Th 1903, p. 3; 23 Tammuz 1906, p. 4.
[9] *TF*, 2 Tammuz 1900, p. 4; 9 Tammuz 1900, p. 4; 7 Aylul 1903, p. 4; Slemman, "Le chemin de fer de Damas," p. 524; *TF*, 15 T al-A 1900, p. 4; 1 T al-A 1900, p. 6.
[10] *TF*, 17 K al-A 1900, p. 4; 26 T al-Th 1900, p. 4; 29 Nisan 1901, pp. 4–5; 11 Ab 1902, p. 4; BBA-Defter.

members of the municipal councils in the Beirut Vilayet sent in substantial sums. 'Abd al-Qadir Qabbani, head of the Beirut Municipality who was also editor of the Pan-Islamic newspaper *Thamarat al-Funun*, gave T.L. 30. The heads of the councils in Tiberias, Nablus, and Tartus donated sums of money. Many local notables serving on city councils contributed T.L. 10 or 20. Another large group of official donors consisted of religious leaders. The muftis of Nazareth, Jeble, Tiberias, and Nablus were among the earliest to donate money. The director of pious foundations of Acre and the head of the sharifs in Nablus gave T.L. 10.[11]

An imperial order from Istanbul required that donations be made by all civil employees of the government. One month's wages were to be deducted from all salaries as a gift to the railroad. This was to be taken in the form of a small reduction from each month's pay. This tax, disguised in the form of a donation, was even applied to Christians; however, the tax on Christian employees was ended in 1902. The civil servants' deduction of 8–½ percent per year was partially ended in 1903. It was retained for officials who made more than T.L. 5 per year; they had to pay 10 percent of one month's salary.[12]

Private Ottoman Donations

The degree to which Ottoman officials exerted pressure, either implicitly or explicitly, to secure donations to the railroad seems to have varied considerably from area to area and time to time. Some gifts were entirely voluntary, others completely the result of official pressures. It seems probable on the basis of the instances discussed below that most of the donations inside the empire were made by individuals and groups with mixed feelings. They felt that presents to the railroad would secure govern-

[11] *TF*, 6 Ab 1900, p. 5; *Donor's List*.
[12] *TF*, 16 Adhar 1903, p. 4; 9 Tammuz 1900, p. 4; Antoine Guine, ed., *Les Communications en Syrie* (Damascus: Office Arabe de presse et de documentation, 1968), p. 35; Angus Hamilton, *Twenty Years in Baghdad and Syria* (London: Simpkin and Marshall, 1916), p. 61; FRA, 319, Savoye (Damascus) to Delcassé, 1 May 1902.

mental approval and at the same time express publicly a personal commitment to Islam. Even where orders were sent out to collect set amounts of funds, donations may still have been at least partly voluntary.[13] However, evidence also exists of widespread complaints and resistance. The collection of donations came to meet with the same opposition that taxes of all kinds encountered in the Syrian area, where the most detailed information concerning gifts is available.

French observers witnessed several cases of forced contributions made in parts of Syria. District governments established minimal contribution schedules from their areas. They arbitrarily fixed amounts for each village, including Christian villages. Local irregular police were used to collect money. They withdrew from recalcitrant villages only when contributions were made. In still another case a set amount of money was taken from the inhabitants of some Syrian villages. Local notables in the villages kept part of the donations.[14]

Less evidence is available concerning forced donations in towns than in villages. Indirect evidence of pressure for donations exists for Beirut. Beirutis who gave donations jointly received separate certificates showing that they had paid and could not be asked to do so again. In Latakia donations were tied to the area's tax yields. Local committees established quotas according to wealth. Under pressure for immediate funds the vali of Beirut ordered that the tax records of all those who were not poor or physically infirm should be examined to see if they had already given to the railroad.[15] In some instances where information is available concerning the circumstances under which donations were given, there is less evidence of overt pressure.

The larger private donors inside the empire were officeholders or former officeholders. The three chief groups of contributors

[13] Slemman, "Le chemin de fer de Damas," pp. 531–32.

[14] Tresse, *Le pèlerinage*, pp. 302–4; FRA, 319, Savoye (Damascus) to Delcassé, 1 May 1902.

[15] F.O. 78/5452, De Bunsen (Constantinople) to Lansdowne, 23 November 1900; *TF*, 15 Tammuz 1901, p. 4; C.E.B., "Notes sur le Panislamisme," *Questions diplomatiques et coloniales*, 28 (1909), 646; F.O. 195/2075, Drummond-Hay (Beirut) to De Bunsen, 22 November 1900.

were the officeholding urban notables, landowners, and merchants. Little pressure was directly applied to these men. The
groups maintained their powerful positions in part by such gestures as giving money to charitable and religious causes. Donations to the Hijaz Railroad achieved a number of purposes. They
supported the sultan's own project, thereby gaining favor with
Istanbul. Contributions were also a means of publicly displaying
generosity, piety, and Ottoman patriotism. Insofar as the background of the donors is known, it appears that the amounts given
were in direct relation to the status of the giver. The leading
notables contributed the most.

Some examples of private donations permit an evaluation of
the circumstances surrounding the gifts. The Beirut merchants
'Abbud and Halbuni, whose trade was with Istanbul, gave T.L.
2,000 to the railroad, on condition that a certain fraction of the
total would be sent in for every 100 kilometers actually completed. They received decorations from the sultan for their generosity. 'Ali Bey al-Katib, an Istanbul merchant, and Mahmud
Paşa al-Jazairi, a Damascus notable, imitated the Beirut merchants' caution in providing a sum for every 100 kilometers finished. The former mufti of Aleppo, 'Abd al-Qadir al-Jabiri, gave
T.L. 50.[16]

Donations were made upon special occasions. While on the
pilgrimage of 1903–4, Ahmad Bey al-Ziyya gave about T.L. 10.
Hasan al-Nabulsi died and left T.L. 160 to the Hijaz Railroad in
his will. The wife of Makki Bey of Thessaloniki, who was of
Syrian origin, left the railroad T.L. 100. A candy vendor in Damascus gave a part of his profits to the railroad. Even Christian
groups and individuals contributed. The rival of the Hijaz Railroad, the French-owned Damas, Hama et Prolongements Railroad, presented the Beirut donations committee with T.L. 84.[17]
The Sunni Beirut newspaper, *Thamarat al-Funun*, was particularly active in soliciting contributions.

[16] *TF*, 5 T al-Th 1900, p. 4; 20 Ab 1900, p. 5; 23 Tammuz 1900, p. 5; 7 K
al-A 1903, p. 7.

[17] *TF*, 8 T al-A 1900, p. 8; 11 Ab 1902, p. 4; 5 T al-Th 1900, p. 4; 23
Haziran 1902, p. 3; Slemman, "Le chemin de fer de Damas," p. 525; Bliss,
"The Sultan's Dummy Railway," p. 734.

An example of the difficulty in evaluating the intentions of the donors was the action of the Lebanese Christian journal, *Lubnan*. It reprinted the arguments of the Greek Orthodox bishop of Beirut, Jerasmius, who urged Christians to give to the railroad. The newspaper then went on to urge that all those who loved their country strengthen the state. In particular, the construction of the Hijaz Railroad was a means of obtaining economic growth for the Ottoman Empire.[18]

Although most of the donors are not identifiable by name or occupation, it is possible to gather some idea of the support of the railroad by piecing together evidence in a few of the empire's provinces, especially the vilayet of Beirut.

The first year of the campaign for collections was the most important since the railroad needed money immediately in order to begin construction. Unfortunately for the provincial collectors, until construction was actually going on and had made discernible progress, skeptics in the Muslin community could label it only a paper project.

Pledges were made by some provincial governors even before they began to receive any donations. The valis of the Beirut, Aleppo, and Syria vilayets promised to send in T.L. 40,000 each. Bursa pledged T.L. 75,000, and in the Hijaz the large sum of T.L. 200,000 was promised. Some idea of the scope of these pledges can be gained by comparison to the budgets of the vilayets. "Private" donations that were pledged from the vilayet of Syria amounted to nearly one-tenth of the yearly tax receipts of that province. Between July 1902 and June 1903 few of the vilayets sent in much money. Bursa supplied T.L. 16,245; Aydın Vilayet T.L. 13,000; but Syria, Beirut, and Hijaz provinces together ontributed only about T.L. 6,000.[19]

Effectiveness in collections depended upon the composition of the committees which solicited them. These committees served as intermediaries between the central government and the local

[18] Slemman, "Le chemin de fer de Damas," p. 525; *TF*, 9 Nisan 1906, p. 6; 30 Nisan 1906, p. 4; 3 Aylul 1906, p. 4.

[19] Tresse, *Le pèlerinage*, p. 303; F.O. 78/5452, Richards (Damascus) to O'Conor, 29 October 1900; BBA-Defter.

Muslim communities. They resembled other groups that apportioned taxes to individuals. This bringing together of representatives of the government and local notables made the process of extracting donations easier. However, it is only in Beirut that the membership of one of the collection committees is known. It consisted of Yahya Bey al-Shim'a, the commissioner of the gendarmerie; Muhammad Efendi Mustafa Bayhum, a distinguished notable; Khalil al-Hisami, the chief clerk of the city council; and Khalil al-Barbir, employed at the Port of Beirut. A different committee was formed during the second major campaign for funds in 1906. The vali was its chairman. The members were the secretary of the vilayet, the director of records, and a member of the Court of Appeals. The first donors in the second campaign were the head of the Sharifs, the mayor of Beirut, and the director of the Post Office.[20]

Similar committees were formed in the vilayets of Aleppo and Damascus. In Medina the shaykh of the Prophet's Mosque headed the campaign for donations. Fragmentary evidence suggests that the other vilayets followed the same precedure.[21]

The geographical distribution of donors in the vilayet of Beirut in both campaigns suggests that they were concentrated in those urban areas where Muslim ruling and commercial groups were numerous. Of the total of 643 donors in the Beirut Vilayet, only 389 can be identified with some certainty, though about 250 more may be assumed to be from the city of Beirut. If this is true, about 585 of the 640 donors came from seven towns: Beirut, 430; Nablus, 39; Tyre, 30; Sidon, 27; Acre, 23; Tripoli (Lebanon), 15; Latakia, 11. Non-Beiruti small donors are considerably underrepresented in these figures. A large but indeterminate number, including possibly some of those attributed to Beirut, came from towns and villages in Mount Lebanon.[22]

---

[20] *TF*, 18 Haziran 1900, p. 5; 22 Tammuz 1901, p. 4; 12 Adhar 1906, p. 4.

[21] *TF*, 11 Haziran 1906, p. 7; 23 Nisan 1906, p. 8; 12 T al-A 1903, p. 4.

[22] *Donor's List* and the following for the second wave of contributions in the Beirut Vilayet: *TF*, 23 Nisan 1906, pp. 5–6; 26 Adhar 1906, p. 5; 14 Ayyar 1906, p. 3; 21 Ayyar 1906, p. 6; 28 Ayyar 1906, p. 3; 18 Haziran 1906, p. 6; 2 Nisan 1906, p. 5; 7 Ayyar 1906, p. 5; 30 Nisan 1906, p. 6; 16 Nisan 1906, p. 3; 9 Nisan 1906, p. 6.

Donations outside the Ottoman Empire

The coercion that marked donations inside the Ottoman Empire did not exist in areas beyond the reach of the sultan's police. It may be assumed that the reverse was the case; colonial regimes put barriers in the way of those seeking to make donations.

Donation campaigns occurred in areas where Ottoman diplomatic representation existed. Ottoman diplomats served as channels for making contributions and in some cases, notably in India, took an active part in soliciting them. Other causes of large-scale contributions were the presence of numbers of Ottoman or former Ottoman subjects, usually traders; the campaigns launched by Pan-Islamic newspapers; and the activities of religious orders, especially the Naqshbandi.

Donations to the Hijaz Railroad illustrate the nature and extent of Pan-Islamic sentiment outside the Ottoman Empire. More importantly, the importance and meaning of the railroad to Muslims throughout the world can be examined in the arguments used for making gifts and the extent of donations. Foreign gifts, however, may have composed only about 8 percent of the donations.[23]

The largest number of collection committees was in India.[24] Indian subjects replied quickly when, as in June 1908, the railroad said it needed money urgently. Through the correspondence of several of the leaders of the donation campaign, the ways in which money was collected and the nature of the appeals used to secure it can be ascertained.

Starting in July 1900 Muslims began to contribute funds to the Hijaz Railroad. The three leading agents in organizing these collections were the Sayyid 'Abd al-Haqq al-Azhari from Baghdad, Abd al-Qayyum of Hyderabad, and Muhammad Insha Allah.

'Abd al-Haqq, the imam of the Manarat Mosque in Bombay, became interested in the Hijaz Railroad in September 1900. He

---

[23] My calculations based on 1902–3 only; see BBA-Defter.

[24] For a sketch of the history of Pan-Islam in India before 1900, see Aziz Ahmad, *Studies in Islamic Culture in the Indian Environment* (Oxford: Clarendon Press, 1964), chap. 4, "Pan-Islamism and Modernism."

had been gathering money for religious works to be printed in
Egypt. After hearing the news of the sultan's appeal from Abd
al-Qayyum, he translated the appeal for funds into Urdu. The
appeal was sent to merchants, notables, and religious men in
Hyderabad. After corresponding with the Ottoman consul in
Bombay, he received certificates in both Ottoman and Urdu. He
hoped to obtain for the railroad the funds set aside every year by
the nizam of Hyderabad to help pilgrims.[25]

The arguments 'Abd al-Haqq used for contributions were
based upon an appeal to Islam and group loyalty. In a speech
given at Amritsar to a Muslim literary club he argued that
Abdülhamid II was the commander of the faithful and the imam
of all Muslims. His project of a railroad to Mecca was a service
to all Muslims around the world, a benefit to both faith and nation. As a result all Muslims and their governments should support the railroad. "My brothers, the equal of this work has not
been undertaken . . . [before; because in the Ottoman Empire]
there is a lack of ability to borrow capital." As a result the sultan
had to appeal for donations if his desire to serve the pilgrims was
to be realized. Those who gave "demonstrate the perfection of
their faith," for "to present gifts for the realization of the Hijaz
Railroad is to demonstrate the love of God and His Prophet." In
addition, "This line is the one way to protect the Hijaz from
Christian threats." 'Abd al-Haqq ended his speech by appealing
to the Indian Muslims to uphold their reputation for generosity.[26]

Abd al-Qayyum wrote to *al-Muayyad* of Cairo as well as *Thamarat al-Funun* telling of his life in the Deccan, where he had
worked for the nizam's government. He was dismissed from one
post in 1900 at the suggestion of the British. *Lisan al-Hal*, a Bei-
ruti newspaper, referred to him as being the leading servant of
the Hijaz Railroad because of his extensive traveling and letter
writing on its behalf. He gained permission from the government of India to collect money for the railroad and founded a
number of committees for that purpose. The first was in My-

[25] *TF*, 17 Aylul 1900, p. 2.
[26] F.O. 78/5452, De Bunsen (Constantinople) to Lansdowne, 23 November
1900; *TF*, 19 T al-Th 1900, pp. 1–2.

sore, where in one week he claimed to have collected more than
T.L. 50. In 1903 he founded collection committees in Madras
and Malabar.[27]

Abd al-Qayyum spoke on behalf of the railroad to a meeting
held in December 1900. He said to the assembled religious men
and newspapermen that the Hijaz Railroad was a "religious and
national project." "By means of this Railroad God has gathered
together the major resources of life in agriculture, commerce,
and manufacturing [for the people of Syria]." Most importantly,
"The pilgrimage will be made easier and the three great mosques
linked."[28]

Muhammad Insha Allah, born in 1870, became a newspaper
editor in Amritsar and later in Lahore. He claimed to be the
originator of the idea of the Hijaz Railroad as well as the leading
fund raiser in India. A profuse correspondence with most of the
major newspapers of the Arab lands and the press of Istanbul
testified to his activities. The two newspapers he edited, *al-Wakil*
of Amritsar and *al-Watan* of Lahore, were strongly Pan-Islamic.
Both conducted appeals to their readers for donations to the Hijaz Railroad. Though pro-Ottoman, Insha Allah protested his
loyalty to the government of India. He urged upon the Ottomans a change in their foreign policy which was, he felt, too
subservient to Germany. By March 1904 he had collected about
T. L. 963 for the railroad. By 1910 Insha Allah had sent in a
total of nearly T.L. 6,500.[29]

There is no information now available concerning other railroad propagandists in India. Several are known to have gone
there from Ottoman lands. The qadi of Medina also served as a
channel of information about the railroad by supplying Indian
pilgrims with donation certificates and news of construction.[30]

[27] *TF*, 9 Shubat 1903, p. 6; 7 K al-A 1906, p. 1.

[28] *TF*, 14 K al-Th 1901, p. 2.

[29] Insha Allah, *History*; *TF*, 2 Tammuz 1900, p. 2; 21 Adhar 1904, p. 5;
FRA, 325, C. Bonin, "Le chemin de fer du Hedjaz," pp. 155–56; FIP, 10,
Nicault (Calcutta) to Ministry, 23 June 1908; I.O. 2848/10, clipping from the
Homeward Mail, 11 June 1910.

[30] *TF*, 15 Tammuz 1901, p. 2; 17 Adhar 1903, p. 3; F.O. 78/5452, Richards
(Damascus) to O'Conor, 15 December 1903.

Although the total amount contributed in India is not known, between July 1902 and June 1903 only about T.L. 4,000 were sent. There is, however, some information on the areas where contributions were made. Over 150 committees were formed after 1900. Of this total nearly 100 were established in the Deccan, where the Muslims were a ruling minority. Other committees existed in all parts of India—the area directly ruled by the British, the princely districts, Burma, and Ceylon. The number of committees continued to grow until 1908. In addition to the committees founded by the three chief fund raisers there was a committee in Peshawar; the secretary of the Ottoman Consulate in Bombay helped set it up. Other organizations were formed in Rangoon, Benares, Kanpur, Patna, Madras, Karachi, Delhi, and Bihar.[31]

Examples of individual donors may suggest the type of Indian who was susceptible to an appeal couched in Islamic and pro-Ottoman terms. There is detailed information only for a small number of cases. Mirza Ali of Calcutta was a large donor who gave T.L. 5,000. Two Kashmiri shawl merchants, the brothers Habib Allah and Ghulam al-Din of Amritsar, gave about T.L. 37. The newspaper *Riad* of Lucknow gathered over T.L. 2,000 for the railroad. Arif Ismail Bihram, a merchant of Calcutta, donated about T.L. 1,000.[32]

Europeans saw the donations as reinforcing the identification of the Ottoman Empire as the defender of Islam. There were doubts about the loyalty of Indian Muslims in the event of a war between England and the Ottoman Empire. The unreality of these fears was demonstrated during World War I, when there were almost no manifestations of Pan-Islamic sentiment. Even before 1914, however, Muslims in India had been reluctant to

---

[31] Kurd 'Ali, *Kitab*, III, 188; *TF*, 15 Tammuz 1901, p. 4; F.O. 78/5452, clipping from the *Oriental Advertiser*, 28 June 1901; Eleftériadès, *Les chemins de fer*, p. 167; *TF*, 26 T al-A 1903, p. 4; 30 Nisan 1906, p. 4; FRA, 325, Bonin, "Le chemin de fer," pp. 155–56; BBA-Defter.

[32] Kurd 'Ali, *Kitab*, III, 188; Samuel G. Wilson, *Modern Movements among Moslems* (New York: Fleming Revell, 1916), p. 74; *TF*, 3 K al-A 1900, pp. 1–2; F.O. 78/5452, clipping from the *Levant Herald* of 6 October 1903; *TF*, 19 T al-Th 1900, p. 5; 7 K al-A 1903, p. 1.

allow the sultan to manipulate Islamic symbols for Ottoman political and diplomatic purposes. For this reason the ruler of Hyderabad, a leading Muslim prince in India, made his pledge to the railroad of over T.L. 20,000 conditional upon the arrival of the railroad at Medina. Indians were interested primarily in the Mecca-Jidda and Mecca-Medina parts of the projected Hijaz Railroad system. When pilgrims landed at Jidda from India, they would use only those parts of the railroad. The sections north of Medina were of little direct help to Indian pilgrims. Because of this lack of interest and the extremely scattered data concerning donations, it seems likely that Indian claims about donations were exaggerated. Total donations were probably between T.L. 17,000 and T.L. 40,000. The lower figure includes all the money definitely known to have been contributed, while the higher number allows for unrecorded gifts.[33]

Ottoman governmental efforts to secure collections were limited to giving certificates and dealing with the government of India. In December 1900 Indians asked for about T.L. 10,000 worth of certificates to be printed in Urdu and sent to India. The supply was increased in 1901 when the Central Committee of the Hijaz Railroad sent several shipments of certificates to the Ottoman Consulate in Bombay. The local Ottoman consul was the chief official contact between the fund raisers in the region and the railroad.[34]

Although the government of India agreed to permit contributions to be made, British officials in Istanbul opposed the decision. The English ambassador in Istanbul, Nicholas O'Conor, thought it likely that the money would be diverted to other purposes. The Ottoman ambassador in London, Musurus Paşa, asked the British foreign minister in October 1903 to give permission to Indian subjects to wear the Ottoman medals, which

[33] *TF*, 7 K al-A 1903, p. 1; FIP, 10, Martin (Bombay) to Pichon, 2 September 1907; Nicault (Calcutta) to Ministry, 22 May 1908.
The records of the Turkish Embassy in London contain a great deal of information on collections both in India and England; however, I have been unable to consult them. My thanks to Bernard Lewis for mentioning them to me.

[34] *TF*, 17 K al-A 1900, p. 4; 24 K al-A 1900, p. 5; 8 Nisan 1901, p. 4; 15 Tammuz 1901, p. 2; 2 T al-Th 1903, p. 4.

acknowledged gifts to the Hijaz Railroad. Both the foreign minister and the India Office opposed this request. Medals were, however, sent covertly to India.[35]

Some Indian Muslims regarded the railroad as a help to Islam, but the probable level of donations suggests that this view was not widespread. The railroad was presented by its spokesmen in India as a part of the Ottoman Pan-Islamic movement. For believers in the political unity of all Muslims, the sultan as the leader of the most powerful independent Muslim state deserved the support of all of the faithful. The chief financial incentive of Indian Muslims who wished to make the pilgrimage was the improvement of their transport. As long as the Jidda-Mecca-Medina section was unbuilt, interest in the railroad was low and contributions were few and scattered.

The second area where extensive contributions campaigns are known to have existed is Egypt. Egypt was nominally part of the Ottoman Empire and paid tribute to it annually. However, by the accession of 'Abbas II in 1892 effective Ottoman political power had not existed in Egypt for many years. The family of Mehmet Ali and the British occupation forces divided political control. In the three-way struggle between the ruling family, the occupiers, and a new group of liberal nationalists, the remaining attachments to the Ottoman Empire were used as a means of gaining popular support. Either of the two Egyptian forces could pose as being pro-Ottoman and Pan-Islamic.[36]

The khedive 'Abbas II began contributions by giving matériel to the railroad for its construction. A central committee for donations was formed with Husayn Paşa Kamil of the khedivial service as chairman. Activity in Gharbiya Province was particularly great. The local committee there was headed by Ahmad

[35] F.O. 78/5452, O'Conor (Constantinople) to Lansdowne, 29 January 1901; F.O. 78/5452, Lansdowne's Aide Mémoire of 21 October 1903; Lansdowne to Musurus Paşa, 30 January 1904; I.O. 254, Viceroy to Foreign Office, 7 January 1904; I.O. 2777, *Levant Herald*, 28 May 1904.

[36] For an examination of Egypt in this period see Robert Tignor, *Modernization and British Colonial Rule in Egypt, 1882–1914* (Princeton: Princeton Univ. Press, 1966).

Paşa al-Manshawi, who later headed the committee for all of Egypt. For his own part he gave more than T.L. 2,500.

A number of Egyptian newspapers supported the campaign for donations. In Zagazig Ahmad 'Abd Allah Husayn, the editor of the local *al-Siba*, began a campaign for contributions in 1900.[37]Other newspapers supporting the railroad were published in Cairo. These included *al-Muayyad* and *al-Liwa*, whose editor was the nationalist Mustafa Kamil. *Al-Muayyad* collected over T.L. 1,000. *Al-Liwa* gained the approval of the khedive for its support of the Hijaz Railroad. Sultan Abdülhamid awarded Mustafa Kamil the rank of mirmiran for his efforts. By April 1904 he had gathered over T.L. 3,000. His brother, 'Ali Kamil Bey, raised T.L. 2,000 in 1908. *Al-Raid al-Misri* wrote that the Hijaz line had in the Muslim world the importance of the Suez Canal in the economic world. Rashid Rida argued in *al-Manar* that a general love for God and his prophet could be manifested in a desire to protect the House of God in Mecca and the tomb of the Prophet in Medina. Making access to both easier, as well as defending them, was a duty for all Muslims. Bishara Taqla, the editor of *al-Ahram*, wrote in favor of the Hijaz Railroad.[38]

Large donors in the early period included an employee of the Egyptian department that sent the covering for the Kaaba to Mecca, a merchant, an inspector of pious foundations, and the head of the sharifs of Tanta.[39] There is no information concerning other individuals.

Donations in Egypt were typical of those made in other semi-independent and colonial Muslim states, such as Bukhara. The

[37] *TF*, 6 Ab 1900, p. 5; 20 Ab 1900, p. 5; 13 Ab 1900, p. 5; 13 Tammuz 1903, p. 4.
[38] "Kayfiyyah jama'a i'anah sikkah hadid al-Hijaz," *Al-Manar*, 6 (1903), 355; Muhammad Rashid Rida, "Mahabbat Allah wa rasulihi fi i'anat al-sikkat al-hadidiyyat al-hijaziyyah," *Al-Manar*, 3 (1900), 362–63; Tresse, *Le pèlerinage*, p. 301; *TF*, 5 T al-A 1903, p. 4; 4 Nisan 1904, p. 5; 11 Nisan 1904, p. 4; FRA, 325, Collomb (Damascus) to Pichon, 10 September 1908; *Al-Ahram*, 31 July 1899, cited by Leon Zolondek, "*Al-Ahram* and Westernization," *Die Welt des Islams*, 12 (1969), 182–95.
[39] *TF*, 16 Tammuz 1900, p. 2; *Al-Manar*, 6 (1903), 280; *TF*, 7 K al-Th 1901; 19 Ab 1907, p. 4; 28 K al-A 1903, p. 4; BBA-Defter.

Muslim leader endorsed the railroad. Then the leaders of the
community made contributions. Collections were organized by
newspapers, Naqshbandi shaykhs, and merchants.

Such campaigns led to clashes with the colonial power. The
railroad as a symbol of allegiance or friendship with the sultan-
caliph was unacceptable to a Christian state. In Egypt the collection of gifts was not officially halted, but participation by Egyptian officials was discouraged. The Ottoman government suggested that Egyptians should contribute five kuruş per person—
the same tax imposed upon Ottoman Muslim households. This
was opposed by the British. At the insistence of Lord Cromer,
Egyptian government employees were forbidden to belong to the
committees set up in Cairo, Alexandria, and the rest of the country to collect money. The civil service was admonished to avoid
any sort of pressure upon the people of Egypt to secure donations. It is impossible to estimate at the present time the effectiveness of the collection campaign, for the total amount donated
and the details of the individual donations are still largely unknown.

Despite the paucity of information on donations in India and
Egypt and the scattered data on gifts in other parts of the world,
it seems clear that at least some money was sent from all parts of
the Muslim lands. Insofar as this was the case, the Hijaz Railroad became more than just an Ottoman railroad. It was the
property of all the world's Muslims. The Islamic interest in the
cities of the Hijaz was broadened to include the Muslim-owned
means of transportation leading to them.

Publicity

One of the steps undertaken by the Ottoman government to promote donations was the publicity surrounding the celebrations
held to commemorate the opening of each section of the railroad.
The opening dates were made to coincide with the sultan's accession anniversary. By this means they gained a symbolic importance and were linked with the ruler personally. Even more important was the evidence these ceremonies provided to skeptics
that the railroad was actually being built. It put to rest fears that

the donated money was not going for its specified purpose. This news was relayed to the Muslims of the world by Ottoman, Indian, and Egyptian newspapers.

The opening in 1908 of the hurriedly constructed last section of the line to Medina was covered by newspapers and journals all over the world. As in the previous ceremonies, many correspondents' expenses were paid by the Ottoman government. Telegraph lines owned by the imperial government were used by reporters without cost. The ceremony in 1908 was marred by the upheaval in Istanbul, which limited the powers of the sultan and posed a potential threat to his Pan-Islamic ideas. 'Izzat Paşa, the leader in the construction of the Hijaz Railroad, was removed from power and exiled; his name was not mentioned during the ceremonies. Nevertheless, the celebration in Medina was seen as being one of a series that had not yet ended. Though the line itself was never to reach south of Medina, the ceremony ended with a cry of "on to Mecca" by the assembled crowd.[40]

Taxes and Other Involuntary Payments

From the beginning of the Hijaz Railroad project it was clear that the empire could not raise enough money through donations. The income was both too irregular and too small. In an attempt to gain new sources of revenue, the sultan created two new major taxes, intended solely for the railroad. They affected nearly everyone in the empire. The first was a poll tax of five kuruş on all male Muslim heads of families. It yielded about T.L. 100,000 per year. The second tax was a special stamp tax, probably modeled after the postal and fiscal stamp taxes issued for aid to immigrants starting in 1901. Revenue stamps of varying denominations had to be attached to a number of types of documents. Some foreigners objected to paying the taxes. The Lynch Steamship Company protested at Baghdad in 1903. In an iden-

[40] "Istanbul 'dan Medine'ye," *Hayat* (Istanbul), 12 (20 July 1967), 34–35; Augustus Ralli, *Christians at Mecca* (London: Heinemann, 1909), pp. 260 and 63–64; Tresse, *Le pèlerinage*, p. 332; al-Marawani, *Al-Khatt*, pp. 17–18; *TF*, 21 Aylul 1908, p. 1.

tical verbal note of 13 March 1903 the European powers rejected
the validity of the stamp tax, demanded its suspension and the
repayment of all money collected from foreigners. However, the
tax continued to be collected.[41]

Another source of income was the recoinage of money from
the vilayets of Tripoli (Libya) and Yemen. Also the obligation to
perform corvée labor on highways was converted into cash payments in Nablus and Acre. The income derived from this con-
version went to the Hijaz Railroad. To provide ready cash for
the railroad's account, T.L. 100,000 was borrowed from the Ottoman Agricultural Bank. By 1908 this sum was increased to
nearly T.L. 486,000. Since the capital of the Agricultural Bank
was derived from taxes, the "loan" from the bank was, in effect,
another tax. Money also came from the customs revenues of Beirut.[42]

Starting with the pilgrimage of 1900–1901 a tax was collected
from every pilgrim who was not too poor to pay it when landing
at Jidda. Payment was graduated according to the area from
which the pilgrims came. The professional guides collected the
money and gave it to the amir of Mecca, who sent it on to Istanbul. In 1903–4 the caravan leaving Medina for Egypt and Syria
was halted until everyone had paid this tax.[43]

Another of the sources of revenue for the railroad was the sale
of the skins of animals slain on the festival of al-Adha. After the
approval of the şeyhülislam in Istanbul, the Council of State sent
orders to the vilayets to form committees in every municipality
to be headed by the mufti of the area. In 1901, in one of the few

[41] F.O. 78/5452, Richards (Damascus) to O'Conor, 15 December 1903; al-
Madi and Musa, *Tarikh al-Urdunn*, p. 15; Peake, *History of Jordan*, p. 97; *TF*, 29
Haziran 1903, p. 4; 7 K al-A 1903, p. 7; 20 Haziran 1904, p. 4; "Taqrir hawla
al-wad' al-shar'i li al-khatt al-hadidi al-hijazi," mimeographed (Damascus,
1964), p. 3; Young, *Corps*, V, 282–84; "Sikkah hadid al-Hijaz wa daribah laha
jadidah," *Al-Manar*, 5 (1903), 877; *TF*, 9 Shubat 1903; 16 Adhar 1903, p. 4; 26
Ab 1903, p. 4; F.O. 78/5452, Newmarch (Baghdad) to O'Conor, 3 and 5 October 1903.
[42] *TF*, 28 T al-A 1900, p. 4; Slemman, "Le chemin de fer de Damas," p.
533; F.O. 78/5452, Richards (Damascus) to De Bunsen, 29 October 1900.
[43] Ibrahim Rif'at Paşa, *Mirat al-haramayn*, I, 71–72; F.O. 78/5452, Devey
(Jidda) to O'Conor, 11 April 1901; *TF*, 8 Tammuz 1901, p. 3.

cases where the results of the sales are known, committees in the Hijaz conducted sales that yielded T.L. 1,000. The total derived from this source in 1901 was T.L. 40,000. The sales were repeated in following years.[44]

Abdülhamid granted the Hijaz Railroad Central Commission concessions at various times. Initially they yielded little revenue but were of considerable promise for the future. They placed natural resources close to the railroad beyond the reach of foreign concessionaires. The grants included lands in Haifa, Acre, and Nazareth; the mineral baths at El-Hamma; the right to generate electricity from the Yarmuk and Jordan; expansion of the ports of Haifa and Jaffa; and the property of the French road company that had operated coaches between Damascus and Beirut. Mineral rights within twenty kilometers of each side of the line were awarded to the railroad.[45]

Total Revenues

The income of the Hijaz Railroad that came from donations amounted in January 1909 to T.L. 1,127,894 out of a total revenue of T.L. 3,975,443. This was about 28 percent of the total income. In previous years donations had formed a much higher part of total income: 1903, 63 percent; 1904, 55 percent; 1905, 35 percent; 1906, 35 percent; and 1907, 32 percent. This decline was paralleled by a decrease in the total sums donated each year. The amount given from the start of the appeal in 1900 until the end of 1901 was about T.L. 417,000. In the next two years there was an increase of nearly T.L. 329,000. In 1904–5, on the other hand, only about T.L. 74,000 was given. The second campaign

[44] *TF*, 25 Adhar 1901, pp. 4–5; 3 Haziran 1901, p. 7; 10 Haziran 1901, p. 4; 8 Shubat 1904, p. 4.

[45] "Taqrir," pp. 8–9; United Arab Republic, Directorate General of the Hijaz Railroad, "Résumé of the stages of the entry of the Hijaz Railroad into participation in the hot mineral springs" (in Arabic), mimeographed (Damascus, 1960), p. 1; F.O. 195/2165, Drummond-Hay (Beirut) to O'Conor, 2 May 1904; M. Blanckenhorn, "Die Hedschaz-Bahn auf Grund eigener Reisestudien," *Zeitschrift der Gesellschaft für Erdkundes zu Berlin*, (1907), p. 224; Peake, *History of Jordan*, p. 97.

Table 1. Types of income

Types of income	1903	1904	1905	1906	1907	1908
Gifts	651,184	742,153	738,616	884,482	1,028,773	1,127,894
Agricultural Bank	150,000	150,446	253,777	303,993	419,992	485,993
Conversion of Currency	165,531	251,439	359,665	369,991	393,078	402,893
Taxes	—	192,217	551,120	920,548	1,236,905	1,648,692
Operating income	—	—	34,690	61,903	133,428	225,310
Corvée	—	—	12,234	14,675	19,237	24,133
Total	1,033,465	1,326,370	2,054,570	2,532,376	3,188,690	3,975,443

NOTE: For 1903 and 1905–7 the figures cited cover the period ending in July; 1904 is the fiscal year 1903–4, which ended in March 1904; 1908 extends to 18 January 1909. Sources are TF, 14 Aylul 1903, p. 3; 18 Nisan 1904, pp. 1–2; 18 Aylul 1905, p. 1; 17 Aylul 1906, p. 4; 9 Aylul 1907, p. 4; "Taqrir," [Hijaz Railroad] *Hicaz Demiryolunun 1324 Senesi . . . Varidat ve Masarifatına . . .* (Istanbul: N.p., 1909?). All figures are listed in Ottoman pounds. The totals have not been adjusted to include costs of the exchange of money. Small sources of money are not included. Because of this, the figures do not comprise the sums listed under "Total."

for contributions, which began in 1906, took in during the next three years T.L. 308,000.[46]

There is no evidence of substantial contributions for the period after 1908. After the completion of the line to Medina, income came from operating revenue, special allocations for capital expenditures, and taxation.

The Significance of Donations

While the cost of the railroad was great, the money voluntarily given was comparatively small. All donations, including those that were forced, were less than one-third of the total income of the railroad in 1908. They became even less, proportionately, as capital expenditures mounted during the period after 1908. In comparison to the total budget of the empire the donations were not large. Ottoman government income in 1890–91 was about T.L. 17,767,000. It rose during the next fifteen years until by 1905–6 it was about T.L. 21,274,000.[47] The average of donations between 1900 and 1908 was only around 3 percent of one year's income. On the other hand, the indebtedness of the Ottoman Empire and the scarcity of ready cash made the donations welcome in financing construction.

The central financial administration of the railroad was capable and honest in achieving the central government's goals. Given the hasty formation of the collection agencies, their success showed that the Ottoman bureaucracy was capable of being flexible and efficient when sufficiently pressed.

Coercion played a great part in internal collections. Spurred on by the central government, local officials felt compelled to supply money rapidly to Istanbul. Government bureaus provided, in all probability, more money than the provinces did. It can be assumed that many Ottoman internal donations reflect no identification with the railroad or its purposes, since they were forced. However, in some cases donations were voluntary. These

[46] *TF*, 12 Aylul 1904, p. 4; 14 Aylul 1903, p. 4; 17 Aylul 1906, p. 4; 9 Aylul 1907, p. 4; Guthe, "Die Heschasbahn," p. 26; Hermann Schmidt, *Das Eisenbahnwesen in der asiatischen Türkei* (Berlin: Siemenroth, 1914), p. 129.

[47] Feis, *Europe*, pp. 313–16 and 335–36; Shaw and Shaw, *History*, II, 226.

became a means, similar to charity, to express personal piety. As a result, the railroad may have seemed to a certain degree to belong to the Muslim community of the empire in general rather than just the dynasty or government.

Donations to the Ottoman sultan for the Hijaz Railroad strengthened the empire's ability to resist European military might. At the same time, the railroad improved the conditions of the pilgrimage. Donations in such areas as India and Egypt were seen by local Muslims as a way of increasing the strength of the Ottoman Empire and displaying public loyalty to the Islamic community at the same time. They implied by these gifts a recognition of the Ottoman ruler as the leader of all Muslims. The donation campaign was important as an example of the way support for a state could be gained by an appeal to traditional religious loyalties. It emphasized the link between the sultan as defender of the Holy Places in Medina and Mecca and his role of ruler of the Ottoman Empire. All of the emotions and attachments associated with Pan-Islam became attached to the Hijaz Railroad. It was the only embodiment of the movement.

The fact that the empire was at last compelled to seek other sources of income for about two-thirds of the railroad's cost was not publicized at the time, although the railroad's financial statements were published. To most of those who were aware of the railroad, its existence was a sign that the Ottoman Empire was strong without Europeans.

Donations to the Hijaz Railroad played a role in creating the Pan-Islamic movement; that role and the movement itself remain to be fully explored. There is no doubt, on the other hand, that the donations had the result of contributing directly to the construction of the railroad itself. With the addition of taxes and other income, the Ottoman Empire, a state notoriously unable to fund large projects on its own, was able to build the line. The financing of the Hijaz Railroad demonstrated that the Ottoman Empire could mobilize sufficient capital to undertake large-scale public works.

Military encampment

Review of the dismounted camel corps at Tabuk

Soldiers and Bedouins at Mudawwara

Constructing a bridge on the Haifa-Dera branch

A mountainside clearing on the Haifa-Dera branch

The Haifa terminal and port

The statue commemorating the Hijaz Railroad at Haifa

Chapter IV

Operations

THE FUNCTIONING OF public utilities once they have been completed is as crucial to understanding the nature of technical development as studies of their purpose, planning, funding, and
construction. Major public utilities controlled by non-European
states face a new range of challenges when they become opera-
tional. The goals of autonomy and efficiency come into conflict
with pressures for foreign control.

An examination of the operations of the Hijaz Railroad measures the ability of the Ottoman Empire to overcome such challenges. The range of skills necessary to operate a large, techni-
cally demanding, and complex organization such as the Hijaz
Railroad was great. The basic issues that had arisen in the funding and construction phases were carried over to operations: the
need for efficient and inexpensive management; the desire to be
independent of foreign advice, advisors, and control; and the
best way to utilize the railroad to achieve increased military and
economic capacity.

In the period following the deposition of Abdülhamid II in

1909, growing Ottoman nationalism increased demands for a policy of autarchy. During the construction of the Hijaz Railroad it had been necessary to allow foreign administrators to deal with technical problems. Foreign skilled labor had been employed. If the Ottoman Empire was ever to become truly independent of foreign control, it was essential to train experienced Ottoman technical personnel of all types, from skilled workers to administrators. This desire to Ottomanize personnel and at the same time gain technical training came into conflict with the desire to have the railroad run as efficiently as possible. Giving priority to the goal of efficient management had the advantage of fulfilling immediately some of the initial reasons for building the railroad. It would increase military mobility, ease the burdens of the pilgrimage and thus help secure domestic and foreign enthusiasm for the regime, and extend governmental control over South Syria and the Hijaz.

The specific way the operations of the Hijaz Railroad tended to meet these desiderata can be seen by examining the major aspects of the railroad's activities between 1908 and 1914. Since railroad records are unavailable, it is necessary to piece together evidence on behavior in each area. Even when official sources are available, their data are frequently unreliable or pertinent only to financial affairs. Hijaz Railroad documents deal with such topics as the amount of freight carried, civilian and military passengers, and the income and expenditures of the railroad. Travelers' accounts, local newspapers, and foreign observers' reports add some detailed information on administration, personnel, maintenance, military movements, and passenger and freight operations.

Central and Local Administration

The vicissitudes undergone by the Istanbul Central Commission during the years following the ouster of Sultan Abdülhamid II were numerous. In brief, it was successively placed in a number of different governmental departments, generally headed by men who probably knew nothing about the railroad and lacked any desire to interfere with its management. Another factor making for local autonomy in the administration was uncertainty concerning the eventual fate of the railroad. Doubtful issues included the extension of the line to Mecca and Jidda, construction of other branches in Palestine toward Egypt, competition with the Damas, Hama et Prolongements Railroad, and the D.H.P.'s desire to gain control of part of the line. All of these problems tended to receive little attention from the central government. It was unsure of its own political stability. Faced with wars with Italy and the Balkan states, the post-Hamidian governments were burdened by diffuse executive leadership. Leadership in the administration of the Hijaz Railroad had originally been centered in the hands of Meissner Paşa and the Damascus Central Commission. After the removal of 'Izzat Paşa al-'Abid, it probably remained in Syria between 1908 and 1914.

The smallness of the Istanbul Central Administration is also an indication of its relative lack of importance. In the expenditures of 1914, for instance, only T.L. 5,991 was spent in Istanbul out of total expenditures of T.L. 221,430. Most of this sum was spent on keeping records. As with other Ottoman government agencies, regulations issued by the Hijaz Railroad insisted on detailed paper work on nearly all aspects of the railroad's operations. Even the tools given to workmen were recorded and the records sent to Istanbul.[1]

Since there is no official information available concerning internal relations between the Istanbul and Damascus sections of the railroad's administration, only suppositions can be made about their exact relationship. The Parliament and sultan retained control over the funding of the railroad, the disposal of its revenues, and the composition of the commissions of the railroad. Extension of the line also depended upon support from Istanbul in the form of large appropriations separate from operating income. The railroad may have maintained internal autonomy through its ability to keep its ordinary, nonconstruction expenditures in balance with its operating revenues. The

---

[1] *Düstur*, 3d ser., (Istanbul: 1911–1917), IV, 519–24; regulations for workers are also available in [Hijaz Railroad], *Hicaz Demiryolu Hareket Nizamnamesi* (Istanbul: Arşak Aruvyan Matbaası, 1327/1909–1910).

Administrative Council of the railroad was interested chiefly in the Ottoman Army's strategic demands upon the railroad since the council was composed largely of military officers. Other members included, however, a representative of the governmental department in which the railroad was located at the time and usually the general director of railroads at the Ministry of Public Works and Commerce.[2]

As construction of the railroad progressed, parts of the line were gradually brought into commercial operation. An operations organization separate from the Construction Administration was first set up in 1905. It was divided along functional lines and by geographical divisions. Freight was directed from Haifa, maintenance and matériel from Damascus, and traffic from the junction station at Dera. This division in authority along functional lines was retained after 1908, but control was centered in Damascus. In the only year when a listing of expenses is available, about 120 people were employed by the local administration, and expenses were about T.L. 80,000 of a total regular budget of T.L. 208,000.[3]

The sections into which the administration was divided were drawn together by a director general. This post was occupied by two Germans between 1910 and 1917. The first of these, Zehringer, had been an engineer on the Anatolian Railroad and head of the technical services of the Ottoman Tobacco Régie. As director he received T.L. 1,600 per year for the two years he held the post. He was replaced by Peter Dieckmann, another German engineer, despite the attempts of the French Embassy in Istanbul to secure a French appointee.[4] The German predominance in operations had been originally balanced by the presence of a French commerce director, Paul Gaudin, who was hired in Au-

[2] *HD-7*, p. 3.

[3] Osman Erkin, "Hicaz Demiryolu," *Demiryollar Dergisi*, 22 (1948), 23; Max Roloff, "Arabien und seine Bedeutung für die Erstarkung des Osmanen reiches," *Länder und Volker der Türkei*, 5 (1915), 113–36; *HD*, p. 3; *HD-7*, p. 13.

[4] FRA, 326, Bompard (Constantinople) to Ministry of Foreign Affairs, 20 April 1910; FRA, 328, Boppé (Constantinople) to Ministry, 19 February 1912; interview with Muhammad Nadim Bey al-Sawwaf in Damascus, 20 November 1969.

gust 1905. He had been dismissed from his former position as director of operations on the Smyrna-Cassaba Railroad because of disagreements with its management. His salary with the Hijaz Railroad was generous; he received T.L. 1,300, which was T.L. 400 more than the Istanbul director made, as well as 3 percent of any operating profits.[5] When his contract expired in 1908 he was not rehired. Gaudin was replaced by Mukhtar Bey, the Ottoman engineer who had been Meissner's assistant in construction.

Personnel

The first problem the operations administration turned to was that of manning its staff and that of the other divisions.

Hijaz Railroad personnel were divided horizontally into geographical districts and vertically into ranks according to status and function. The chief division was between those paid by the day and those on salary. For the latter there was created a table of organization, which did not necessarily have a close relationship to personnel policies because of inability to fill certain posts. Fortunately, a list based on the workers actually paid exists for 1912. At the end of 1912, of the nearly 3,800 people who were employed by the Hijaz Railroad, 2,654 were day laborers, 675 were salaried, and 460 worked by the month. A large majority (516) of the salaried employees were in the Traffic Department; 48 were concerned with new construction and repairs; and only 121 dealt with administrative matters per se. More than one-half (1,737) of the day laborers worked on repairs and new construction; considering the length of the line at this time (1,469 kilometers), this was a low figure.[6] In general, officials involved in the railroad's administration were only about 5 percent of total personnel.

Departmental classifications corresponded to the operations

[5] FRA, 323, Boppé (Constantinople) to Rouvier, 1 August 1905; Erkin, "Hicaz Demiryolu," p. 23; F.O. 195/2190, Drummond-Hay (Beirut) to O'Conor, 1 October 1905.

[6] *HVA-M*; *HD*, p. 3.

areas of the railroad. The major divisions were Administration, Freight, Traffic, and Repairs.

The chief personnel problem involved the hiring of Europeans rather than Ottomans, who were possibly less qualified. In the past the Ottoman government when awarding railroad concessions to companies had included a clause aimed at forcing them to hire Ottoman citizens. An example is in the Mudanya-Bursa Railroad Convention: "All agents and employees of the Railroad other than technical personnel will be chosen among Ottoman subjects; they will wear the clothing which will be prescribed by the Imperial Government; all will wear the fez . . . the Society will employ in its technical operations under equal conditions engineers graduating from the [Ottoman] School of Civil Engineering; . . . all agents and employees other than engineers and administrators must know how to speak Turkish."[7]

The policy of the government had been clear, but it was largely ignored by the concessionary companies. Now that there was an Ottoman-owned and-managed railroad, the policy of employing Ottoman citizens could be applied.

At first this policy remained as much a dead letter for the Hijaz Railroad as for the foreign railroads. The early operations officials were almost entirely Europeans, at least on the higher levels. A German Pole was director of traffic at Dera after 1903; the chiefs of the maintenance squads were foreigners; the controller of finance for operations in 1904 was an Austrian. On the other hand, most of the personnel immediately below these posts were in the Ottoman military. Station masters at Maan, Dera, and Damascus were exceptions: they were Ottoman Christians, former employees of the D.H.P. or the Anatolian Railroad.[8]

While construction was going on, attempts had been made to train Ottomans to replace Europeans. Sultan Abdülhamid had ordered some of the engineers graduating from the School of Engineering and the School of Arts and Crafts to work on the railroad. Students from the latter school had to work five years

[7] Young, *Corps*, IV, 182.

[8] F.O. 78/5451, F. Maunsell, "Reports on the Syrian Railways, 1905," pp. 10–11.

as a minimum, but their education had been free. Engineers were sent every year to Europe to improve their education. When they returned, they went to work for the Hijaz Railroad.[9]

In the period before these efforts could produce qualified personnel, the only Ottomans available were those who had worked on Hijaz Railroad construction or with other railroads in the empire. During the wars and threats of war between 1908 and 1914, military personnel had to be withdrawn from the railroad. The skills needed in the Freight, Administration, and Traffic departments were not the same as those developed in construction. The Maintenance Department and the new construction in 1912–14 presumably did make use of men having these skills.

Until 1912 most of the middle-level personnel in operations departments were Europeans, and a majority were Germans. In a list of the supervisory employees at Damascus the extent of the foreign presence can be seen. All of the following posts were filled by Germans: the general director of the railroad; the traffic director; the head of the Damascus yards and his two assistants; the foremen of the carpenters, fitters, and boilersmiths; the freight car repair chief; and three skilled laborers.[10]

Only on the last section of the railroad, between Madain Salih and Medina, where Christians could not be employed because of their religion, could Muslim Ottomans be reasonably sure of gaining a job with the Hijaz Railroad. However, it was precisely this section that had relatively little importance because of its lack of freight and passengers except during the pilgrimage season.

To counter domination by Europeans, the Ottoman War Ministry suggested that foreigners' contracts not be renewed once they expired. European chiefs of departments were required to obtain permission before hiring foreigners. In the case of the British head of the repair shops at Qadam, his Ottoman subordinates were even instructed to keep his movements under sur-

---

[9] FRA, 325, Bonin, "Le chemin de fer du Hedjaz," pp. 48–49; *TF*, 6 Ab 1906, p. 4; *HD*, p. 19.

[10] FRA, 328, Chiha, commercial agent of the D.H.P. at Damascus, to the director of traffic of the D.H.P. at Beirut, 10 June 1912.

veillance.[11] Some posts, particularly those at the lower level, were held by Ottomans from the beginning of operations. Examples were the central and local administration clerks, locomotive drivers, and telegraphers. By 1914 the al-Sawwaf family of Damascus occupied a number of posts in the technical committees of the railroad. In 1913 Ottoman engineers returning from European educations began to fill posts held by foreigners. During the war the railroad required all of its employees to know Ottoman. Written instructions to workers and administrators were given only in Ottoman. Letters to the railroad could be written only in Ottoman or Arabic.[12]

In the lower ranks of the railroad the exclusive hiring of Ottomans had started earlier and was more successful. By 1905 only two foreign locomotive drivers, both Germans, remained. All the rest were Ottomans who had been recruited from the navy dockyards and other sources. Nearly all these men constituted, however, another problem in that they had to be trained in the technical skills involved in railroad work. The employment of Muslims at the lower level and foreigners at the higher meant that occasionally Muslims were given orders by non-Muslims. Since the former objected to obeying Christians, at times there were conflicts that were resolved only by the supervisors' resigning.[13]

In 1909 there were 163 men working at the Damascus maintenance and engineering depot. Only thirteen were non-Ottomans, but these included the locomotive superintendent (French), the works manager (British), one foreman (French), and two electricians (German). By 1914, on the other hand, all station masters were Ottomans, though most firemen on locomotives were French, Greek, or Lebanese Christians.[14] The number of

[11] Schmidt, *Das Eisenbahnwesen*, p. 129; F.O. 195/2342, Young (Damascus) to Lowther, 24 June 1910.

[12] Personal interview with Muhammad al-Sawwaf, 20 November 1969; FRA, 329, D.H.P. to Ministry, 29 March 1913.

[13] F.O. 78/5451, F. Maunsell, "Report, 1905," p. 11; F.O. 371/350, F. Maunsell, "Report on the Hijaz Railway, July 1907."

[14] Durham, Box 13214, H. Channer, "Report on the Hedjaj [*sic*] Railway,"

Muslims employed on the railroad increased, but higher administrative and some technical posts remained largely the preserve of foreign employees until World War I.

The functioning of the railroad depended upon the conditions of work of its employees to a greater degree than had been the case during construction, when most unskilled labor was done by soldiers. The Hijaz Railroad offered a number of inducements to keep qualified workers. Skilled workers were paid as much as T.L. 5 per month; an apprentice fireman in 1915 made about T.L. 3 per month. This compares favorably with the T.L. 900 per year paid to the Istanbul director of the railroad, who presumably was at the other end of the Ottoman hierarchy of employees. Fringe benefits included cheap housing at Dera for those on the Damascus-Haifa-Maan runs; free transportation on the railroad for workers and their families; and gifts upon marriage, injury, and death. The first retirement funds for state workers ever established in the Ottoman Empire were created in 1911 for the arsenal and Hijaz Railroad employees. A medical service for employees provided free doctors and medicines for workers.[15] On the other hand, major disadvantages for workers were posed by the weather, dangerous Bedouins, and the accidents and hardships attendant upon running a steam locomotive with relatively little experience.

In the short time between 1908 and 1914 the railroad remained dependent upon foreign personnel in key areas, but evidence is available that partially successful attempts were made to train, hire, and improve the working conditions for Ottoman employees.

June 1909, p. 1; F.O. 371/2781, "Report on the Hijaz Railroad," 25 September 1916.

[15] Personal interview with Hasan Nas'a, 13 January 1970; [Hijaz Railroad], *Hicaz ve askeri demiryollar ve limanlar idare-i umumiyesi . . . talimatname* (Istanbul: N.p., 1333/1914–1915), pp. 37–40; Lütfü Erişçi, *Türkiye'de İşçi Sınıfının Tarihi* (Istanbul: Kutulmaş Basımevi, 1951), p. 11; *Düstur*, 3d ser., II, 241–45.

Gifts varied according to the employee's pay, but were generous. For example, the heirs of a worker making T.L. 5 per month would receive T.L. 75 when he died (*Düstur*, 3d ser., VII, 666).

Repairs, Maintenance, and Traffic

The first task for the Repairs and Maintenance Department was to complete the line. Although construction reached Medina in August 1908, a number of facilities necessary to the maximum utilization of the railroad existed only on paper. These included living quarters at most stations, quarantine facilities that would comply with international safety regulations, quays at Haifa to improve freight handling, freight storehouses, water storage tanks, repair facilities, and switching yards at the major stations. Freight and passenger facilities in particular were inadequate. Their construction continued until 1914, but it was not complete even then. By 1914 the railroad had managed to build an adequate system of major station buildings and some traffic facilities at Haifa, Dera, Damascus, Maan, Tabuk, Madain Salih, and Medina.[16]

Another function of the department was maintenance of the existing line. Drainage culverts, which periodically became choked with sand, had to be cleared on a regular basis. If this was neglected, the rare but violent floods resulting from rain storms would destroy embankments. Occasional damage by Bedouins also had to be repaired. Circassians and some settled Haurani Arabs were formed into ten- to fifteen-man crews. Each crew maintained and repaired a ten-kilometer section of track.

The ability to keep engines and cars in running order was even more important to the successful functioning of the line than new facilities. Here the gap between official statements about the railroad and practice contrasted sharply. The slow rise in the number of locomotives and wagons the railroad owned was largely meaningless, since many of them could not be used for any purpose whatsoever. Rolling stock lasted only half of the operating life that European experience suggested was normal.[17]

The problem of maintaining existing rolling stock serves as indirect evidence about the state of technological training of the railroad employees. From the beginning of construction through the whole Ottoman period of control, cars and engines were

[16] *HD-7*, pp. 20–21; *HD*, pp. 33–35.
[17] F.O. 195/2342, Young (Damascus) to Lowther, 24 June 1910.

taken out of operation because of maintenance problems. In 1906, for example, when the railroad had thirty-eight locomotives, seven were totally useless and ten were being repaired. In 1909 only half of the locomotives worked. By 1911 fifty-five of eighty-six were operable. There are some indications that as freight increased, those locomotives that worked were used much more frequently, resulting in depreciation not reflected in the financial statements.[18]

To a certain extent the large number of locomotives under repair or abandoned as irreparable was caused by the extreme climatic conditions of the area, but another cause was the carelessness of drivers and maintenance men. In 1909 the railroad started to fine workers who damaged property; this resulted in better maintenance. Another cause of locomotive malfunctioning was the fuel employed—a mixture of Ereğli (Heraclea) and Cardiff coal. Ereğli coal alone was too smoky. It clogged the steam tubes in the locomotives' boilers. Even with the mixture, engines had to be cleaned after any long trip.[19]

Maintenance had a direct effect upon the efficiency with which the line was run and the services it provided passengers. In the early years maintenance and service to passengers had had low priority compared to finishing construction. Passengers made many complaints about damaged cars and leaking roofs. In one case a freight wagon collapsed because of overloading. A group of Egyptian pilgrims traveling in 1909 mentioned many inadequacies, including lack of first-class wagons, slowness of the trains, and employees who knew no Arabic.[20] On the other hand, occasionally the railroad management showed flexibility in trying to adjust to the needs of its customers. Bedouins who took part in the pilgrimage of 1908 did not want to use the third-class wagons, in part because such wagons had no facilities for sleeping. They were permitted to set up tents on flatcars. Sleep-

[18] Great Britain, *Parliamentary Papers* (Accounts and Papers), 116 (1908) Cmd. 3727, "Trade of Damascus"; FRA, 326, Gaillardot (Haifa) to Pichon, 15 November 1909; *HD-7*, p. 19, has the official statistics on rolling stock.

[19] F.O. 78/5451, F. Maunsell, "Report, 1905"; F.O. 371/350, F. Maunsell, "Report, 1907," p. 8.

[20] FRA, 326, Ribot (Cairo) to Pichon, 17 November 1909.

ing facilities were added to first- and second-class coaches in 1912. A special mosque car with a diminutive minaret six and a half feet high was used on the pilgrimage trains. Christians were accommodated on the trains, though usually they did not go south of Maan. Cook's tours used the railroad from Haifa to Damascus. Partially to please European travelers but also to gain uniformity in timing of schedules, the Hijaz Railroad switched from telling time beginning with sunset to the European method of reckoning time.[21]

Perhaps the most obvious criterion to use in evaluating the operations of the Traffic Division was the ability to run trains on time. Even in using so seemingly simple a measure, care must be exercised to ascertain actual practice and how it differed from the behavior detailed in official documents.

The only known printed timetable of the Hijaz Railroad, dated March 1914, listed the frequency and arrival times of all trains.[22] Two examples are the service from Damascus to Medina, three a week, in fifty-six hours; and the Haifa to Damascus run, seven a week, in eleven and one-half hours. In practice these seem to have been optimal times for both trips. The Damascus-Medina trip took three days usually. In one case in 1911 it took five and one-half days. Haifa-Damascus, according to some travelers, lasted about fifteen hours.[23]

Assuming that the 1914 Hijaz Railroad schedule was correct, the speed attained by trains was low. Over most segments of the line, including short rest stops, locomotives averaged only twenty-five kilometers per hour or less. Of course even at this rate the speed was still faster than that provided by camel caravans or horse-drawn carriages. Before completion of the Rail-

[21] Tresse, *Le pèlerinage*, p. 338; L. Dominian, "Railroads of Turkey," *American Geographical Society of New York Bulletin*, 47 (1915), 938; Karl Baedeker, comp., *Palestine and Syria*, 5th ed. (Leipzig: Baedeker, 1912), p. 143; Mark Sykes, *The Caliphs' Last Heritage* (London: Macmillan, 1915), p. 480; Hecker, "Die Eisenbahnen," p. 1316.

[22] FRA, 332, Haifa to Ministry, 20 April 1914.

[23] Great Britain, *Parliamentary Papers* (Accounts and Papers), 87 (1911) Cmd. 5707, E. Weakley, "Report on the conditions and prospects of British trade in Syria"; *Revue du Monde Musulman*, 6 (1908), 264.

road, the pilgrims spent as much as forty days in getting from Damascus to Medina.[24] The railroad was at least ten times faster.

Passenger Operations

An analysis of the impact of the railroad upon those in Syria and the Hijaz who sought to travel is difficult to make. Available data, found chiefly in official railroad documents, permit only tentative deductions about the importance of passenger traffic to the economic viability of the railroad. The chief passenger users were pilgrims going to Medina; most of the available information therefore pertains to them. Since in the period 1909–14 passenger revenues provided, on the average, one-half of the total income of the railroad, the increase or decrease in the number of passengers, their propensity to travel long or short distances, and the problems encountered in expanding the railroad's pilgrimage facilities affected the overall ability of the railroad to operate successfully.

A slow but continuing rise in the number of passengers was matched by an increase in passenger revenues. Such figures are not necessarily indicative of the type of passenger the railroad served. If the revenue is analyzed by type of ticket purchased, it becomes clear that passengers overwhelmingly bought third-class tickets. First- and second-class tickets from 1910 to 1913 averaged only 5.7 percent of total passenger sales. The rest came from third-class ticket sales. It was only with the introduction of second-class carriages in 1912 that the sales of other tickets increased.[25] Syrian society contained relatively few who could afford to add the luxury of comfort to the luxury of long-distance travel by rail. Excluding pilgrim revenues, the average trip on the railroad apparently cost only about one-third of an Ottoman pound.

At the same time as revenues from passengers were increasing, the distance traveled tended to decrease. For the one year when statistics are available, considerably more passengers rode through

[24] Al-Marawani, *Al-Khatt*, p. 2.
[25] *HD*, pp. 4, 5, and 7.

Table 2. Civil, pilgrim, and military passengers

Year	Number of passengers	Passenger income	Number of pilgrims	Pilgrim income	Number of military	Military income
1908	139,262	—	—	—	—	—
1909	119,033	93,063	19,965	59,860	8,480	—
1910	168,448	139,802	25,079	100,316	77,761	18,466
1911	171,101	175,289	29,102	116,408	27,390	13,134
1912	186,662	167,570	30,062	120,248	47,941	22,546
1913	232,563	184,427	31,416	130,600	43,484	18,885
1914	213,071	95,723	—	—	147,586	122,598

NOTE: All income figures are in T. L. Sources are HD, pp. 4–7; F.O. 195/2311 Devey (Damascus) to Lowther, 2 January 1909; "Die Hedschasbahn," *Archiv für Eisenbahnwesen*, XXXIX (1916), 304, 308–11. Most of the original data are based on the Ottoman financial year from March to March, i.e., statistics for 1908 cover the period March 1908 to March 1909. The revenue from pilgrims, but not that from the military, is included in passenger income.

the well-settled areas served by the 278 kilometers of the line between Damascus and Haifa than between Dera and Medina: 151,862 versus 32,466. Since the rates per kilometer were higher on the latter segment and nearly all passengers rode all the way to Medina, these few passengers provided more money than their numbers would indicate.[26] Nearly all the passengers were pilgrims on their way to the Holy Cities.

The Hijaz Railroad faced a number of barriers to rapid, cheap, and easy transport of pilgrims to the Hijaz even after its completion to Medina in 1908. Most important was the gap between Medina and Mecca.

Travelers from Syria and the Muslim areas north, east, and west of it could choose several possible routes. Only a few of these permitted the use of the Hijaz Railroad. Maghribis and Egyptians could go to Haifa or Beirut by sea and then visit Damascus or Jerusalem. Then they would travel to Medina via Dera.[27] After performing the rites in Medina, they would travel to Mecca by caravan or to Medina's seaport, Yanbu, then by steamer to Jidda-Mecca-Jidda and return to their homes by sea. Anatolians, Syrians, and Central Asians could use the Suez Canal to Jidda-Mecca-Jidda and then go by sea or camel to Medina and north by the Hijaz Railroad. Iranians and Iraqis after traveling overland via Najaf and Karbala and central Arabian oases would visit Mecca, then Medina. The trip north to Damascus and then overland to Iraq was an alternative to the sometimes dangerous southern caravan routes.

The chief competition to the railroad was the sea route to the Hijaz. Since detailed figures were kept on the number of pilgrims coming by sea but not those on land, it is difficult to compare the two. However, preliminary estimates indicate that a majority of those pilgrims who came from outside the Arabian Peninsula arrived by sea from India and Muslim lands to the east of it. These pilgrims were not possible customers for the railroad.

[26] "Die Hedschasbahn," p. 306; FRA, 332, Haifa to Ministry, 20 April 1914.
[27] Landau, *Hejaz Railway*, pp. 49 ff., deals with the pilgrimage ceremonies and the routes from Damascus to Mecca in detail.

In the only year when figures were compiled, about one-fourth of the pilgrims who traveled on the railroad originated in Haifa; the rest started from Damascus.[28]

The railroad charged T.L. 7 for a third-class round-trip Haifa- or Damascus-Medina ticket. This was more than a month's wages for a skilled laborer working on the railroad. For Syrians and those from the north traveling by land, the shipping fare from Beirut was roughly comparable. The railroad's advantage was that it saved the expense of traveling from the pilgrim's hometown to the Mediterranean coast and back and one trip from Medina to Yanbu by camel. The railroad trip was faster, and therefore less money had to be spent on food. Another inducement to use the railroad was that at times the imperial government ordered the line to carry indigent pilgrims free.[29]

In the period 1908–13 the number of pilgrims who came overland with the Syrian pilgrimage doubled that of the time preceding completion of the Hijaz Railroad. Insofar as is known, about 5,000 pilgrims had gone by camel from Damascus to Medina before 1900.[30] By 1913 about 10,000 were going south to Medina and 21,000 north to Damascus more quickly and cheaply than had been possible before.

Every year more pilgrims went north than came south by the railroad. Sometimes there were twice as many. This suggests that many who used the railroad were from the north. Once they had traveled to Jidda-Mecca-Jidda and Yanbu-Medina by sea and caravan, it was advantageous to avoid the dangerous trip back to Yanbu by using the railroad north from Medina. Unfortunately, it is difficult to prove this hypothesis since complete data compiled at the quarantine stations operated by the railroad seem to exist only for 1908, 1909, and 1912.[31] According to this infor-

---

[28] "Die Hedschasbahn," p. 306.

[29] F.O. 618/3, Devey (Damascus) to Lowther, 28 September 1908; F.O. 368/228, Monahan (Jidda) to Lowther, 4 November 1908; *TF*, 6 Nisan 1908, p. 7; *Düstur*, 3d ser., IV, 540.

[30] Landau, *Hejaz Railway*, p. 159.

[31] "Die Hedschasbahn," pp. 308–10; F.O. 368/228, Clemow (Constantinople) to Lowther, 28 November 1908; Rifaat, *Rapport général sur la campagne du*

mation, the main groups of pilgrims using the railroad were, in order of size, Russians and Central Asians, Anatolians, Syrians, Egyptians, Persians, and Iraqis. Since the number of pilgrims in any given year depended to an extent upon economic and political conditions in the country of origin, it is difficult to isolate the new appeal of the railroad from other causes. In order to do this, the absolute number of pilgrims coming by the railroad should be considered as a part of the total number of pilgrims arriving in the Hijaz by all means of transport. For example, about 8,000 Russians and Central Asians made the trip by sea in 1909, and 3,814 came via the Hijaz Railroad. About one-half of those from Syria and perhaps the same proportion from Anatolia who went on the pilgrimage came by the Hijaz Railroad. Since the numbers returning were larger in each case, it seems plausible that the railroad drew most of its customers from Syrian and Anatolian pilgrims on the return trip. Other pilgrims continued to use chiefly the sea routes.

The Hijaz Railroad gained additional passengers as well as prestige from carrying the Egyptian and Syrian mahmals, the camel-borne litters symbolic of temporal authority in the pilgrimage. In at least 1910 and 1911 the route Cairo-Alexandria-Haifa-Medina-Mecca was taken by the Egyptian mahmal in order to avoid certain Bedouin tribes who attacked the caravan of 1908.[32] Another inducement to pilgrims to use the railroad was that the quarantine arrangements established at Tabuk were cheaper and more efficient than the Egyptian quarantine station at Tur in Sinai. However, occasionally the problems of organizing train service for large numbers of pilgrims with only a small supply of rolling stock available overwhelmed the railroad. One example occurred in 1912, when nearly 4,000 pilgrims left Medina via Yanbu because they grew tired of waiting for space on overcrowded trains. On other occasions movement was more

pèlerinage de 1909 (Constantinople: Gérard Frères, 1909), p. 6; Albrecht Wirth, *Vorderasien und Aegypten in historischer und politischer, kultureller und wirtschaftlicher hinsicht geschildert* (Stuttgart: Union Deutsche, 1916), p. 294.

[32] FY, 141, Bertrand (Jidda) to Ministry, 12 March 1908; FPM, 3, Lepissier (Jidda) to Istanbul, 25 January 1911.

rapid. Six thousand pilgrims were transported from the quarantine station to Damascus in about ten days in March 1908.[33]

Troop Movements before World War I

The successful operation of the railroad's passenger service was paralleled by its services for the Ottoman military. The railroad showed itself capable of moving large numbers of soldiers quickly and efficiently. Troops were both more mobile and in better condition once they arrived than had been the case when soldiers who ventured into the areas of South Syria and the Hijaz were dependent upon camels.

The new military capacity of the empire was used while construction was in progress. Ratıb Paşa, vali of the Hijaz, obtained 3,000 men from Damascus to help crush insurgent Bedouin tribes who controlled the area between Yanbu and Medina in 1904.[34] The reinforcements reached Yanbu by using the railroad to Maan and then marching to Aqaba where they embarked on steamers. A similar route was followed by the twenty-eight battalions who were moved from Damascus to Hudaydah, Yemen, in less than two weeks in 1905. During 1905–6 this route was used for sending soldiers to Yemen, thus avoiding the tolls paid at the Suez Canal.[35] Although the intended branches to Aqaba on the Red Sea and from Medina to Mecca were not built, the railroad brought the Arab provinces of Yemen and the Hijaz much closer to major Ottoman centers of military strength.

Another use of the railroad was to help crush rebellions close to its own tracks. The rapid success of the military operations of Sami Bey al-Faruqi against the Druze in 1910 was made possible by use of the Hijaz Railroad in mobilization and transport of troops. Thirty-one battalions were fed and supplied by means of the railroad. Garrisons were maintained along the tracks, but

[33] FRA, 328, Director of operations of the D.H.P. to Beirut, 31 January 1912; F.O. 195/2277, Devey (Damascus) to O'Conor, 11 March and 1 April 1908.

[34] FPM, 2, Dubief (Jidda) to Ministry, 3 April 1904; F.O. 195/2165, Richards (Damascus) to O'Conor, 15 March 1904.

[35] Sait Toydemir, "Hicaz Demiryolu İnşaatı Tarihinden," *Demiryollar Dergisi*, 22 (1948), 67.

there were no attacks on the line.[36] The campaign made possible Ottoman military penetration of the Druze area in Syria. The Hijaz Railroad was soon extended to Busra which it reached in 1913.

Freight Operations

The short period of operations, the vagaries of climate and crops, and the Italian and Balkan wars make it difficult to evaluate the degree to which the Hijaz Railroad met the empire's desire to foster economic growth. However, increased exports and competition with foreign railroads surely existed to a greater degree than before.

As with passenger transportation, there was an increase in the amount of freight handled in the five years 1909–13. Competition for freight business against the rival French-owned Damas, Hama et Prolongements Railroad tested the ability of the Hijaz Railroad to the utmost. Competition between the French and Ottoman railroads centered around a struggle to see which would get more of the wheat sent from the Hauran to the Mediterranean. Because of an Ottoman financial and diplomatic crisis, the French government, acting on behalf of the D.H.P., tried to gain control over the Hijaz Railroad. Only the advent of World War I saved Ottoman control of the railroad. Paradoxically, the growing economic success of the railroad's freight operations proved to be its major enemy by spurring European intervention against it.

The hiring of Peter Dieckmann as director of the Hijaz Railroad in 1910 seems to have revitalized freight operations. Dieckmann, following in Meissner's path, took an active interest in all aspects of the railroad, including its lagging freight business.

Despite the attempts of Rida Paşa, director of the Haifa branch line before 1908, and Paul Gaudin, director of freight for the main line in the early years, the railroad had provided poor service to its early customers. The basic problems were a lack of rolling stock of all kinds, the absorption of men and matériel in

[36] F.O. 195/2343, Devey (Damascus) to Lowther, 30 September 1910.

Table 3. Freight operations

Year	Freight in tons	Revenue in T.L.
1908	—	75,981
1909	76,974	—
1910	65,757	62,224
1911	77,523	70,991
1912	91,626	84,895
1913	112,007	94,062
1914	74,867	80,575

SOURCE: "Die Hedschasbahn," pp. 290 and 304.

construction, the absence of nearly all freight facilities along the line, and the inexperience of the personnel. In the early years trains were often late or unavailable, bribery was needed to avoid endless delays, and there were cases of theft and spoilage.[37] However, the Hijaz Railroad still represented a savings for those merchants or landowners who could ship in bulk.

Starting in 1910 the railroad attempted to secure additional markets and to change its commercial practices to attract smaller shippers. The Ottoman Bank in Haifa was used as a middleman between merchants and the railroad. The bank bought enough merchandise that was landed at Haifa to constitute a full wagonload, thus saving T.L. 5 from the railroad's charges for partial or mixed loads. Once the goods arrived in Damascus merchants took delivery and paid the bank the advance and the railroad the freight charges. The railroad then paid 15 percent of the freight bill to the bank.[38]

Another device used to promote business in 1910 was the special rates given to shippers who sent wheat from Damascus to Benghazi. The first part of the journey on the railroad completed, the wheat filled the empty holds of vessels that had carried Libyan salt to Palestine and had formerly returned empty.

[37] F.O. 371/350, F. Maunsell, "Report, 1907," p. 4; Gertrude Bell, *The Desert and the Sown* (London: Heinemann, 1907), p. 36; Great Britain, *Parliamentary Papers* (Accounts and Papers), 116 (1908) Cmd. 3727, "Trade of Damascus," p. 16.
[38] FRA, 326, Piat (Damascus) to Pichon, 1 December 1910.

In the middle of 1912 Dieckmann sent a group of merchants in Damascus a series of new conditions designed to undercut the D.H.P.'s prices. Most important was an immediate reduction in the price of shipping wheat, from thirty-seven and one-half to thirty-one kuruş per ton per kilometer. In addition he offered the following: free shipment between the Qadam station just outside Damascus and the main downtown station; two tons could be added to "full" loads free of charge; there were special rebates for very large shippers; and a general promise of improved speed and·frequency of service was made.[39] The new series of rates that went into effect in July 1912 were lower for all goods than the prices charged by the D.H.P. An example was salt: ten tons of salt, one wagonload, shipped from Beirut to Damascus by the D.H.P. cost T.L. 14.74; the rate was T.L. 9.74 by the Hijaz Railroad from Haifa. The savings on a ton of sugar were nearly as great. By 1913 small shippers were beginning to buy wheat brought to Haifa from the Hauran on the Hijaz Railroad and take it in sailing vessels to Beirut, where it was cheaper than that coming directly to Beirut by the D.H.P. In addition, special favors were given to the Hijaz Railroad's customers by the customs authorities at Haifa. These in effect lowered costs at the comparative expense of Beirut shippers.[40]

The Profitability and Utility of the Hijaz Railroad

Successful passenger and freight operations can be deduced from the gradually mounting total operating income figures between 1909 and 1913. Despite a series of economic problems caused by wars, disease, and internal uprisings, income of the railroad rose. Although expenses per kilometer rose faster than income, most of the increase can be ascribed to the need for repairing inadequate structures left from the earlier construction, higher costs

[39] FRA, 328, Chiha of the D.H.P. operations, 10 June 1912; for a discussion of similar practices on the Anatolian Railroad, see Quataert, "Ottoman Reform," pp. 202–7.

[40] FRA, 328, Memorandum of the directorate of operations of the D.H.P., 31 January 1912; FRA, 330, D.H.P. to the Ministry of Foreign Affairs, 14 June 1913.

in maintenance of track once the soldiers in the construction crew had stopped work, and normal depreciation.

What would seem to be the most obvious criterion for successful operations, profit, was the most misleading one provided by the financial records of the Hijaz Railroad. The definition of profit as the surplus of income over expenditures in relation to the total capital invested has little to do with a state-controlled economic enterprise. The strategic and developmental goals of such undertakings make profitability less important than it is for private companies. Since the Ottoman government had sources of revenue larger than those of any foreign railroad and was willing to invest money irrespective of its profitability, comparison with the profit of other railroads in the empire would be of little value. It was important, however, that the railroad's nonmilitary operations paid their own expenses. In this it was successful: the Hijaz Railroad did not constitute a drain on the central treasury.

With generally successful performance in each section of the railroad's operations, the formal financial balance sheet of the railroad can be put into perspective as only one indication of overall performance. Much is not reflected in this measurement: the development of an administration that depended upon recruitment of foreign employees for key posts; the more successful attempt gradually to replace European middle-level skilled workers with Ottomans; the operation of new equipment, hindered considerably by the high rate of damaged rolling stock. The sudden and spasmodic military demands for transport in 1905–6 and 1910 were met competently. Passenger and freight development were hindered by the nearly barren countryside covered by the southern two-thirds of the line. Still there was a slight increase in both types of business and particularly in transport of Hauran wheat to Haifa and pilgrims to the Hijaz. There was a great increase in the speed of transportation in the area. Trips that had taken several months were now faster, cheaper, and safer for passengers and freight.

Despite difficulties, the main objectives envisaged by Sultan Abdülhamid and supported by his successors were, on the whole, being met in the operations of the Hijaz Railroad. The military capacity and autonomy of the empire were increased; a

Table 4. Profitability

Year	Total operating income	Operating expense	Operating profit	Capital
1908	225,310	385,777	−160,467	3,473,898
1909	188,963	—	—	—
1910	267,890	197,644	70,246	3,894,071
1911	290,486	208,979	81,507	4,037,527
1912	305,723	251,072	54,651	4,174,886
1913	326,433	244,667	81,766	4,313,574
1914	316,798	221,430	95,368	4,515,829

NOTE: All figures are in T.L. at 100 kuruş per pound. Capital is defined as the total amount spent on the railroad since the beginning of construction, less operating expenses. The table is based on information in *HD*, pp. 4–21; "Die Hedschasbahn," pp. 302–4; *Hicaz Demiryolunun 1324 Senesi . . . Varidat ve Masarifatına . . .* (Istanbul: N.p., 1909?).

beginning was made on training Ottomans who could deal with the administrative, technical, and mechanical problems involved in running a large railroad; and efficient use of the railroad presented a challenge to the increasing foreign economic control of the empire.

The station at Mudawwara

The station at Mudawwara

The station at Maan

A station in the Hauran

The railroad yards and station at Dera

Arrival of a postal train at Maan in the early days of construction

The chief street of one section of Maan

Chapter V

Impact upon Society

THE INTERNAL HISTORY of the Hijaz Railroad can be used as a way of measuring three major issues: the Ottoman Empire's ability to construct and finance a modern enterprise; the efficiency with which the empire could operate such a railroad once built; and the independence of the empire from Europe in personnel, finance, and matériel. The achievement of success in these areas—capacity, efficiency, and independence—was seen by Sultan Abdülhamid and his successors not as an end in itself but rather as a means of achieving political, military, and economic goals in the area of South Syria and the Hijaz. Success in achieving these goals was measured by the impact of the railroad upon the society of the regions it traversed. The Hijaz Railroad's impact may be measured in the following areas: the Bedouin tribes' political independence; settlement and security in East Jordanian towns and villages; and the relationship of Medina with the amirate of Mecca, the Ottoman central government, and the Bedouin tribes.

The Ottoman political goal of centralization was not accompanied by a clear program for using freight and passenger operations to achieve economic growth. The economic impact of the railroad upon towns and villages was unplanned and small, though increasing just before 1914. The economic effect of the railroad upon the inhabitants of South Syria and the Hijaz varied directly with their distance from the railroad's tracks. The settled peoples received the mixed blessings of security, taxes, decreased autonomy, and economic change. For the Bedouin tribesmen the railroad posed the challenge of Ottoman military superiority.

The issue of autonomy was also raised in connection with international quarantine problems and commercial competition. Because of the pilgrims' greater numbers and quicker travel, the empire was obliged to take health measures to guard against the spread of disease. The railroad's competition with the Damas, Hama et Prolongements Railroad was a threat to the growing control of the Syrian economy by French companies. At the D.H.P.'s insistence the French government sought to destroy Ottoman control of the Hijaz Railroad.

Military capacity was tested when the Hijaz Railroad became the chief means of transportation for the Ottoman Army's operations in Egypt and Palestine. The defense of the empire in Syria was largely dependent upon the performance of the Hijaz Railroad.

Political Challenge in South Syria and the Hijaz: The Bedouins

A clear account of the internal history of the Bedouins of Jordan and the Hijaz has not yet appeared. The Bedouins' relationships with the Ottoman state and their connection with the pilgrimage caravans are also nearly unknown. Yet a few basic generalizations can be made about the situation of the Bedouins before the railroad reached them. The most important relates to their economy. In comparison to those living in settled areas, the Bedouin tribes were poor. They were dependent upon herding, occasional irregular agriculture, and some carrying trade for income. Most of the land they inhabited was too dry for raising agricultural crops. A large source of wealth came from settled peoples who owed political and economic allegiance to the tribe or from the pilgrims who passed through the Bedouin areas. Goods were sold to the tribes by traders as well. Merchants went from Damascus and Jerusalem to markets at Muzeirib and Karak. Wheat and other grains came from Northern Syria and the Hauran. Rice, sugar, and coffee were imported via Wajh on the Red Sea. In return for these goods the Bedouins provided camels, salt, and some foodstuffs to traders and pilgrims as well as security from raids.[1]

Relations between the Ottoman government and individual Bedouin tribes were constantly changing. The general structure of Ottoman policy under Abdülhamid II may be seen as one of expansion of central control wherever possible, combined with conciliation of certain tribes when it was temporarily necessary to do so. This policy recognized the fact that Bedouin forces could not resist Ottoman regulars in the desert if the Ottomans made an all-out, expensive, and lengthy attack. However, the Bedouins might at times be able to achieve effective local military superiority because of the scarcity of supplies available to the Ottomans, Bedouin tactical mobility, and the disparity between the expenditures needed for Ottoman expeditions compared to the small resulting increase in tax revenue if they were successful.

Permanent inexpensive military control in prerailroad days depended upon the presence of an agricultural population that could provide revenue, manpower, and transport for Ottoman troops. Yet even where such a population existed, as in the case of the semisedentarized tribesmen of Karak, Madaba, and Salt, they had to be treated with care. Many villagers and townsmen maintained ties with the nomads as well as memories of a period when the Ottoman tax collector did not appear. On the other hand, insecurity of land tenure and incessant inter- and intra-tribal conflicts created a desire among some peasants and townsmen for Ottoman control despite the imposition of taxes and conscription.[2] An example was the Huwaytat tribe, who regis-

[1] Landau, *Hejaz Railway*, pp. 78, 88–89, 168–69.
[2] Peake, *History of Jordan*, p. 86; *MKA–SAH* 1, p. 974.

tered their lands in the name of a tribal leader when the Hijaz telegraph line was built. They were afraid that the land would be taken as imperial property or given to urban notables if it was not registered. From that time on many felt they had an interest in the preservation of the records of land registration, even though they later split on the issues of tribal leadership and policy toward the Ottoman Empire.

The policies used for bringing the tribes under Ottoman control varied from area to area. In the Hijaz the empire relied on the amir to use his authority to mediate between the tribes and the pilgrims. Only on rare occasions did Ottomans fight Hijazi tribes directly. The large detachments of Ottoman soldiers that accompanied the pilgrimage caravans simply guarded the pilgrims from Bedouin attack; they were not used for imposing Ottoman control upon the Bedouins.

In Jordan, Ottoman garrisons were set up in some towns and cooperation with Circassian immigrants was established. Taxes were levied among some of the Jordanian tribes. The head of the tribe set individuals' contributions and received one-fifth of the tax as his own compensation.[3] As with other sectors of the Ottoman population, direct contact between citizens and agents of the central government was avoided. Instead, mediators were recruited among traditional leaders.

The Ottoman policy of seeking to win over the leaders of some of the tribes by alliances, bribes, honors, and supplies was of long standing. Yet it seems to have worked with only limited success even when the government's goal was only that of achieving freedom of transit. When the empire expanded its goals to include local stability and security, it came into conflict with the tribal leaders. As a result, recourse was had by the Ottomans to direct military occupation. When this was impossible, an individual leader who could control large numbers of subtribes was supported by the Ottomans.

An example of the application of these policies can be seen in the history of the Rashid dynasty, paramount chieftains of parts

[3] Interview with Shaykh Turki, a member of the Sakhr tribe, 24 January 1970.

of the Shammar tribe. The long reign of Muhammad ibn Rashid (1869–1897) witnessed his domination of most of Central Arabia. Following his death a confused period of struggle between various members of the ruling clan ensued. In 1905 Ottoman troops joined with Rashidi forces in a campaign. The Ottoman policy of supporting the Rashidis was maintained through the next five years. Honors were conferred on their tribal leaders, and military supplies were sent to the Rashidi capital at Hail. In 1910, however, an Ottoman garrison was requested by the people of Tayma. The Rashidi regent, Zamil ibn Rashid, occupied the village and killed the pro-Ottoman faction. He continued a raid against the Wuld 'Ali tribe even to the point of occupying temporarily their headquarters at Madain Salih on the Hijaz Railroad.[4] Ottoman-Rashidi friendship was based on mutual antipathy toward enemies and the lack of a common frontier rather than shared values or delegated power.

An example of a tribe generally unfriendly to the empire was the Huwaytat from 1908 to the end of World War I. 'Arar ibn Ghazi, the chief leader of the Huwaytat, had opposed the Ottoman advance to Maan in 1894. He was arrested and held at Karak for two years. When he returned to his tribe, he discovered that his authority had disappeared. After 'Arar's death Ottoman support helped his son, 'Awdah Abu Tayyah, achieve an insecure paramountcy. 'Awdah initially welcomed the railroad. The Huwaytat participated in registration of land. 'Awdah's rule was partially based on Ottoman subsidies for guarding the pilgrimage and, later, the railroad.[5] However, as a result of the killing of two tax collectors during a dispute, 'Awdah was outlawed in 1908. Ottoman support then shifted to 'Arar's son, 'Abtan. Subsequently 'Abtan joined the allies of the Ottomans, the Rashidis, in an alliance. In this way the Huwaytat was split into two parts with most support behind 'Awdah and the policy of opposing the Ottomans. During World War I 'Awdah joined the Arab

[4] F.O. 195/2198, Hussein, Memorandum, in Devey (Jidda) to O'Conor, 23 March 1905; Alois Musil, *The Northern Negd* (New York: American Geographical Society, 1928), p. 248; idem, *The Northern Hegaz* (New York: American Geographical Society, 1926), pp. 154–55.

[5] Musil, *Northern Hegaz*, p. 7.

Rebellion, became one of the leaders of the Bedouin contingent of the Arab army, won the admiration of T. E. Lawrence, and helped blow up the railroad he had formerly been paid to protect.

The first direct result of the construction of the Hijaz Railroad upon Ottoman-Bedouin relationships was financial. Although the nature and amount of the yearly payments by the pilgrims to the tribes has not yet been fully established, the continuation of the payments was essential to the safety of the pilgrims. Since the railroad was being constructed in order to replace the caravans, the question arose as to whether the Ottomans would continue payments to the tribes on behalf of the pilgrims.

This issue became more pressing as the railroad came closer to Medina. The 'Atiyya and Huwaytat had concluded an agreement with the Constantinople Board of Health for the protection of the quarantine lazaret at Tabuk. It seemed to be difficult to convince the railroad to continue the payments for protection of the pilgrims. The history of the fighting around Medina in 1908–9, which will be discussed presently, was closely connected with the issue. Its financial result was the imposition of a special surcharge on passenger tickets from Madain Salih to Medina. Proceeds amounted to T.L. 16,876 in 1910. After March 1911 a new method of collection based on distance traveled south of Dera was instituted. Proceeds were given to the tribal shaykhs every month for allocation to the tribesmen.[6]

The Ottoman official position was that payments to the Bedouins were to recruit extra guards. In fact, the money deterred tribesmen from attacking the railroad. Despite the promise of income from this source, the tribes at times felt it was necessary to take strong action to secure the delivery of the payments. An example occurred in Maan in 1910 when payment was extorted from a local Ottoman official by Huwaytat horsemen.[7]

Other economic benefits to the Bedouins provided by the Hijaz Railroad included selling milk, cheese, and meat to the soldiers working on construction; occasionally renting camels to

---

[6] *HD*, p. 5; *HD*-7, p. 8; Interview with Turki, 24 January 1970.
[7] Musil, *Northern Hegaz*, pp. 9–10.

contractors; and the opportunity to steal from the railroad. Wooden sleepers were replaced in many parts of the line with steel ones because Bedouins stole them to use as firewood. There is no indication that tribesmen worked as laborers on the line.[8]

The political impact of the Hijaz Railroad upon the tribes varied according to their distance from the line. The tribes that dominated the southern sections of the line were the following: from Amman to Qatrana, the Sakhr; from Jurf ed-Darawish to al-Ramla, the several clans of the Huwaytat; al-Ramla to al-Mu-azzam, the 'Atiyya; al-Muazzam to al-Ula, the Fuqara; between al-Ula and Hadiyya, the Wuld 'Ali; south of Hadiyya and around the city of Medina, the Harb were predominant. Between Medina and the Red Sea the Billi tribe was in control.[9] The Hijaz Railroad found it convenient to treat these territorial divisions as permanent and generally acceptable to all the tribes. But this was simply not true. Because tribal mobility was so great, disputes over grazing and water rights were numerous. Before the railroad was begun, changes in pilgrimage payments had been forced on the Ottomans by the tribes conducting raids on the caravans. The leader of the land pilgrimage paid those tribes that seemed to him to be the greatest danger to the pilgrims. With the coming of the railroad the tribes attempted the same tactics. During construction most tribes had posed no danger to the railroad. Circassians and Haurani Arabs in maintenance crews along with the troops doing construction work provided security against raids. Two infantry companies were mounted on camels for protection of the telegraph and railroad. Apart from putting stones on the tracks, the Bedouins did not cause any delay in construction. However, acquiescence by the Bedouins to the railroad's construction was not the same as approval. The large tribal groups opposed the railroad; by 1907 the

[8] Durham, "The Hedjaz Railway"; *TF*, 16 Tammuz 1906, p. 7; Muhammad Kurd 'Ali, "Sikkah," pp. 973–74; F.O. 78/5451, F. Maunsell, "Report on the Syrian Railways, 1905."

[9] "Die Hedschasbahn," p. 300; Great Britain, Admiralty, Naval Intelligence Division, *A Handbook of Arabia* (London: H.M.S.O., 1916), I, 47, 56; Douglas Carruthers, *Arabian Adventure* (London: Witherby, 1935), pp. 21–22; Musil, *Northern Hegaz*, p. 22.

ʾAtiyya, Harb, and Billi were, at the least, unsympathetic to it.
Ottoman reinforcements had to be sent to the garrison near
Maan in early 1907 to guard against attacks by the Sakhr.[10]

In 1908 Bedouin opposition to the railroad mounted to the
point of open rebellion against the empire. There was an uprising near Medina. It was related to Hijazi politics, the relations
between the amir and the central government, and the conflict
over revenue from pilgrims.

When the Hijaz Railroad began to approach Medina, the amir
ʾAli and Ahmed Ratıb Paşa, the vali of the Hijaz, let it be known
to the tribes that they were opposed to the railroad.[11] To this
secret encouragement the Bedouins added their own fear of the
railroad's competition with the camel caravan trade. They
thought they would lose revenues from camel sales and protection of pilgrims. Kazim Paşa, then still the chief local Ottoman
supervisor of construction, came to Medina to push forward the
building of the railroad in the Hijaz. Fearing opposition by the
Bedouins, he ordered the arrest of several tribal leaders. When
Kazim left Medina for Rabigh on 10–11 January 1908, the first
tribal uprising broke out. Part of the ʾAwn section of the Harb
attacked Kazim's 1,000-man cavalry escort. Despite his successful passage through the Harb attackers, the Yanbu-Medina route
was closed to travelers. Only after Kazim released the leaders at
the order of Istanbul was the route temporarily reopened. Even
then it was not safe. The Egyptian mahmal was soon thereafter
attacked near Medina, and the rebellion began to spread.[12]

In May 1908 the cycle of arrests of tribal leaders by the Ottomans followed by Bedouin raids culminated in an attack by
tribesmen on Medina. Most of Medina's Ottoman garrison was

[10] F.O. 78/5451, F. Maunsell, "Report, 1905"; *TF*, 1 Nisan 1907, p. 4; Auler, *Die Hedschasbahn*, pp. 40–41; Najib Saliba, "Wilayat Suriyya, 1876–1909,"
Diss., Michigan, 1971, p. 293; *Al-Ahram* (Cairo) 1 July 1904, p. 1; *TF*, 27
Haziran 1904, p. 3; F.O. 371/350, F. Maunsell, "Report, 1907," p. 12; F.O.
371/350, F. Maunsell (Constantinople) to Gleichen, 28 March 1907.
[11] F.O. 371/539, Hussein (Jidda) to Lowther, 22 September 1908.
[12] F.O. 371/539, Monahan (Jidda) to O'Conor, 3 February 1908; FY, 111,
Bertrand (Jidda) to Ministry, 12 March 1908; F.O. 195/2320, Monahan (Jidda)
to Lowther, 27 March 1909.

working on the rapidly approaching railroad. The vali appealed to local citizens to aid the 200 remaining soldiers. Fearing the results of a Bedouin occupation, Medina civilians fought against the tribesmen. Reinforcements from the railhead reached Medina only on the eleventh. The fighting then spread to Hadiyya which was 170 kilometers north of Medina. It was attacked by the Bedouins, who were repulsed. Eight battalions of troops from the Fifth Army came to the railhead north of Medina as reinforcements. The total troop concentration there was about 6,000. By July these reinforcements and the mobility provided by the nearly completed railroad allowed the Ottomans to defeat the Masruh section of the Harb in two battles. The leaders of the rebels were arrested.[13]

The events in Istanbul in 1908 that weakened Abdülhamid's power resulted in the downfall of the sharif and of the vali of the Hijaz. The tribes blamed these officials for their own opposition to the Hijaz Railroad. In return for acceptance of the railroad the Ottomans agreed to restore payments formerly given to the tribes.

The ensuing uneasy peace was broken when the tribes resumed fighting near Medina in November 1908 because the subsidies were not paid. Caravans were raided again. Three thousand troops were sent to Medina by train. It was only with the arrival of a new Ottoman governor for the city that an arrangement was concluded to permit the Syrian mahmal to leave Medina. The Syrian pilgrims agreed to pay high prices for camel transport from Medina, with the proceeds going to the tribes that had begun the fighting.[14]

Although large-scale fighting between Bedouins and the army ended in 1908, a constant series of small attacks was made on the railroad. About 130 incidents of robbery, assault, or attack were recorded in 1908 after the conclusion of peace. The Wuld 'Ali, Juhaynah, Hawazim, Ahamidah, and eventually parts of the

---

[13] F.O. 371/539, Monahan (Jidda) to Barclay, 29 May 1908; FY, 111, Bertrand (Jidda) to Pichon, 28 May 1908; F.O. 371/539, Barclay (Constantinople) to Grey, 25 May 1908; F.O. 195/2277, Devey (Damascus) to Barclay, 18 May 1908; F.O. 195/2286, Hussein (Jidda) to Barclay, 30 July 1908.

[14] F.O. 371/767, Monahan (Jidda) to Lowther, 20 January 1909.

Huwaytat joined in raids later. The railroad's service was disrupted north of Medina from the middle of January to 10 February 1909. To avoid delays, many pilgrims used the sea route.[15]

The relative peace that ensued between 1910 and 1914 was partly due to measures taken to strengthen the defenses of stations. All stations south of Madain Salih were given barbed wire fences, trenches, earthworks, and garrisons of troops. Another cause of peace was the prompt payment of subsidies. It became clear to the tribes that with the increased mobility of regular Ottoman troops, the railroad itself could not be attacked and permanently held. On the other hand, it became clear to the Ottomans that their troops were unable to maintain military superiority far beyond the railroad's tracks. Although the extension of Ottoman authority now had reached the villages from which the Bedouins had derived their revenue, the tribes themselves remained beyond the reach of troops. It was only internal Bedouin divisions that promised the Ottomans a future further erosion of tribal autonomy.

During the first two years of World War I the same pattern that had existed before 1914 was continued. Subsidies were paid to the tribes to guard the railroad. Sa'ud ibn 'Abd al-'Aziz, the leader of the Rashidis, was supported by means of supplies transported on the railroad line. In August 1917 he made Madain Salih his headquarters.[16] In 1917 and 1918 the military success of the British and the ending of Ottoman subsidies persuaded most of the Bedouin tribes to attack the railroad. The Ottomans did not supply the Bedouin requirements of food, fodder, and money because of the difficulty the Ottoman Army experienced in transporting goods on the Hijaz Railroad. Military supplies sent to Ottoman forces provided tempting loot for Bedouin raids, especially when normal sources of income had disappeared.

---

[15] F.O. 618/3, Devey (Damascus) to Lowther, 28 January 1909; F.O. 195/2320, Richardson (Jidda) to Lowther, 30 August 1909; F.O. 368/338, Hussein (Jidda) to Lowther, 19 May 1909.

[16] *AB*, no. 46, 30 March 1917, p. 143; *AB*, no. 66, 21 October 1917, p. 410.

Political Change in South Syria and the Hijaz: The Towns

As the few towns in South Syria near the railroad grew in size and importance, Ottoman control began to expand, reaching outward from Dera, Amman, and Maan. Since autonomous villagers and sedentarized nomads lacked the mobility of the Bedouins, they could be brought under effective Ottoman control with the coming of the Hijaz Railroad.

One example of the railroad's impact upon a town occurred during the rebellion of Karak in 1910. Karak was about fifteen kilometers from the nearest Hijaz Railroad station, Qatrana. Karak had a population of between two and three thousand in 1910. The tribes who lived in the town were dominated by the al-Majali clan, whose chief, Qadar al-Majali, was elected to the Administrative Council of the Syrian Vilayet in 1910. When the vali of Syria refused to accept his election, Qadar Bey began to plan revolt. However, it was Ottoman expansion in the form of conscription, confiscation of arms, the census, and land registration that won the bulk of the townspeople and neighboring tribes over to his rebellion. These measures had been enforced in the Hauran by the Ottomans after their defeat of the Druze. The Karak area seemed to be next.[17]

When the Karakis rose against the Ottomans, they were soon joined by tribes in the area. The Sakhr had not received their subsidy of about T.L. 4,000 for guarding the railroad. They robbed a train, killed some railroad workers, and destroyed sections of track. The 'Atiyya tribe attacked the railroad near Maan. Qatrana station was destroyed; the railroad employees there were killed, rolling stock was damaged, and rails were taken up.[18]

The immediate Ottoman military response was limited because many railroad cars were on the southern side of the break

[17] Madi and Musa, *Tarikh al-Urdunn*, pp. 18–20; Peter A. Gubser, *Politics and Change in al-Karak, Jordan* (London: Oxford Univ. Press, 1973), pp. 106–10.

[18] Sykes, *Caliphs' Last Heritage*, pp. 471–74; Barru, *Al-'Arab wa al-Turk*, p. 215; *HD*, p. 24.

in the tracks and consequently could not be used to transport troops from Damascus to Karak. After a delay of eight days the track was repaired, troops were sent to Karak, and the revolt suppressed. The Karakis had killed Ottoman officials and destroyed government property. When the town was taken by Ottoman troops, they carried out executions, arrests, and looting. Karak was rapidly brought under Ottoman control through the transport of troops on the Hijaz Railroad. The damage done to the railroad by the tribes was estimated at about T.L. 80,000.[19] Given an opportunity to challenge Ottoman power by a town revolt, the Bedouins of South Syria attacked the property and personnel of the Hijaz Railroad.

Next to Damascus, Medina was the largest city on the Hijaz Railroad network. It was part of the Hijaz Province before 1908. Effective political power in the Medina area was then divided among three major groups—the representative of the amirate of Mecca, the Bedouins, and the Ottoman government. Ottoman officials in Medina were the governor, the judges and judicial advisors, the head of the police, and the commander of the small Ottoman garrison. The governor also acted sometimes as guardian of the Prophet Muhammad's tomb at Medina. The representative of the amir supervised all court cases involving Bedouins. Although the power of the Ottoman officials in Medina before 1908 is not yet clearly known, it has been established that there were few or no taxes levied by the Ottomans. Conscription and land registration did not exist. In 1903 the attempt by the Ottoman governor to impose a street-cleaning tax resulted in riots. Disturbances in 1904 showed the garrison to be unreliable because it had intermarried with inhabitants of the city. After a mutiny of part of the garrison in 1906, the guardian of the Prophet's mosque, Osman Ferid Paşa, was appointed governor. He had been a key figure in local politics as the chief Ottoman representative in the city for fifteen years.[20]

---

[19] F.O. 618/3, Devey (Damascus) to Marling, 13 December 1910; Madi and Musa, *Tarikh al-Urdunn*, p. 23; F, 114, Gueyrand (Jerusalem) to Pichon, 15 December 1910; F.O. 195/2370, Devey (Damascus) to Marling, 11 January 1911.

[20] 'Ali Hafiz, *Fusul min tarikh al-Madinat al-Munawwarah* (Jidda: Shirkat al-

As the construction began to near the Hijaz, a series of meetings was held in Medina. The guides' guild decided to encourage the pilgrims they escorted to use the railroad. At the suggestion of the religious authorities, some notables are said to have volunteered to work for one day at the railhead. Nearly sixty Medina merchants rode to Damascus on a special tour in 1907 in order to examine the railroad's operations. A station building was put just outside the walls of Medina. Both the station and the Prophet's mosque were illuminated by electricity in 1908.[21]

The extension of Ottoman control that construction of the railroad made possible had several results for Medina. It was separated from the Hijaz Vilayet and made a separate governate. The Ottoman central government stated that Medina was now directly under the Ministry of the Interior, not the Hijaz Vilayet. On the other hand, in the same telegram the traditional rights of the amirate in Medina were reasserted. Although little evidence is available concerning administration in these years, the division of responsibility in religious appointments at least remained the same. After 1908 the central government established two government schools and a local branch of the Committee of Union and Progress. The foundation of a college in the city was announced in 1913; it was opened in 1914.[22]

During World War I the railroad had the greatest effect upon the people of Medina.[23] By making possible the successful Ottoman defense against Arab attacks, the railroad enabled the Ottomans to withstand a siege whose severity nearly destroyed the town. In early 1917 about one-half of the civilian population was

Madinat al-Munawwarah li al-Taba'ah, n.d.) pp. 36–37; Ibrahim Rif'at Paşa, *Mirat al-haramayn*, II, 105–6; F.O. 195/2174, Hussein (Jidda) to O'Conor, 23 May 1904 and 31 July 1904.

[21] *TF*, 27 Ab 1906, p. 4; 20 Ayyar 1907, p. 7; al-Marawani, *Al-Khatt*, p. 17; A. J. Wavell, *A Modern Pilgrimage to Mecca* (London: Constable, 1918), p. 79.

[22] Al-Batanuni, *Rihlah*, p. 253; Abdullah, King of Transjordan, *Memoirs* (London: Jonathan Cape, 1950), p. 89; *Al-Muayyad* (Cairo), 23 April 1910; Hossein Kazem Zadeh, *Rélation d'un pèlerinage à la Mecque en 1911-1911* (Paris: Leroux, 1912), pp. 22–23; F, 123, Couget (Beirut) to Doumergue, 17 December 1913; *Düstur*, 3d ser., V, 319–22.

[23] Naci Kıcıman, *Medine Müdafaası Yahut Hicaz Bizden Nasıl Ayrıldı?* (Istanbul: Sebil Yayınevi, 1971) presents the Ottoman story of the siege of Medina.

forced to go north on the Hijaz Railroad in order to reduce the drain on the city's food supplies. By February 1918 nearly all civilians had been expelled. Many of the houses were destroyed in order to provide fuel for the railroad's locomotives. Widespread looting followed the entry of the Bedouins when the Ottoman forces surrendered Medina on 10 January 1919.[24]

Political Change in South Syria and the Hijaz
The Amirate of Mecca

The balance of political powers in the Hijaz Vilayet did not change because the railroad reached Medina. The decisive change was caused by the Revolution of 1908 in Istanbul. The decision was then taken to oust the amir, the vali, and the governor of Medina. The Sharif Husayn ibn 'Ali was installed as amir in December 1908. Husayn acquired predominance in 1909–10 in Mecca, Jidda, and Taif after he crushed the small branches of the Committee of Union and Progress there. He was able to force the dismissal of governors with whom he disagreed. A series of alliances with Bedouin tribes was arranged. Of the four newspapers that came into existence after the restoration of the Constitution in 1908 only one, which Husayn controlled, endured. Ottoman garrisons in all of the Hijaz totaled no more than 5,000 men in 1910. The net effect of the Revolution of 1908 in the Hijaz was that the new amir gained more power.[25]

In public the amirs had favored the construction of the Hijaz Railroad. Privately they may well have feared that its continuation to Mecca would decrease or even eliminate both their political and economic power. There is some evidence that the Amir 'Awn al-Rafiq prompted Bedouins to attack the Hijaz telegraph line.[26] The amirs' opposition to the railroad was supported by the Istanbul enemies of 'Izzat Paşa. When the Vali Ratıb Paşa's papers were examined after his overthrow in 1908, correspon-

[24] *AB* no. 45, 23 March 1917, p. 125; *AB*, 31 May 1917, p. 250; *AB* no. 62, 8 September 1917, p. 369; Musa, *Al-Husayn ibn 'Ali*, p. 141.
[25] FY, 142, Lepissier (Jidda) to Ministry, 20 September 1910; F.O. 195/2350, Monahan (Jidda) to Lowther, 7 June 1910.
[26] FP, 131, Guès (Jidda) to Delcassé, 20 April 1902.

dence with several of the sultan's favorites, including the minister of the interior, was discovered. The vali had been encouraged by 'Izzat's enemies to oppose the southern extension of the railroad. Support for the extension came from the Sharif 'Ali Haydar, a member of another branch of the Hashimite family of sharifs. He was a competitor for the amirate. His views may have been intended to curry favor with the central government.[27]

In 1914 the issue of building the railroad was revived by the vali, Vehib Bey, who wished to bring the Hijaz under the new Law of Vilayets. He discharged many officials and made hints of more reforms to come, including imposing taxation for the first time. The Bedouins rose in rebellion and cut communications between the Red Sea coast and Mecca and Medina. Six battalions of troops were sent from Damascus to Medina. When the dissatisfaction at Vehib's orders led to riots in Mecca, the grand vezir ordered the vali to back down. A mob had gone to the Ottoman headquarters in Mecca where it protested against the Vilayet Law and the Hijaz Railroad while praising the Amir Husayn. Fearing an urban and Bedouin uprising, the vali and the amir jointly sent a telegram to Istanbul asking for instructions. They suggested that peace could be restored if the Hijaz Railroad extension were to be abandoned, there was no conscription in the Hijaz, and the amir's court in Jidda were to retain jurisdiction over all Ottoman citizens. Immediately after receipt of the telegram approving these points was made known in the Hijaz, commerce was resumed between Jidda and Mecca. Peace was rapidly restored.[28]

While Vehib Bey was attempting direct means to bring the Hijaz under Ottoman control, Talat Paşa, the minister of the interior, embarked upon a parallel attack of his own. He said to the Sharif 'Abd Allah, a son of the amir, that his father would be deposed if he opposed the Hijaz Railroad. If the amir decided to support the extension, the government would agree to put the

[27] *TF*, 7 Aylul 1908, pp. 4–5; 14 Aylul 1908, p. 2; Stitt, *Prince of Arabia*, p. 123.

[28] Abdullah, *Memoirs*, p. 109; FY, 144, Ottavi (Damascus) to Doumergue, 31 March 1914; FY, 144, De Rettel (Jidda) to Ministry, 22 March 1914.

railroad under his control. The terms were that Husayn and his sons would be guaranteed the amirate; T.L. 250,000 would be given the sharif for distribution to the Bedouin tribes; military forces used in construction would be under the amir's orders; and one-third of the railroad's income would be given outright to the amir.[29] World War I intervened before the project could be carried beyond initial discussions. By 1914 the centralist regime that controlled the empire seemed determined to impose its control first on Medina and then on the rest of the Hijaz. The Hijaz Railroad would have been its chief tool in achieving this goal.

Economic and Social Development: Towns and Villages

The geographical area the Hijaz Railroad traversed was divided sharply between districts where agriculture, and therefore settled life, was possible and the desert or semidesert, where rainfall was inadequate to grow crops. The impact of the railroad was probably greater in the oases and tribal encampments located in the latter area than in the towns. However, even such a generalization as this is based upon evidence too scanty to permit anything more than suggestions of the general nature of social and economic change caused by the railroad.

The railroad's business was greatest in the agricultural areas of Palestine and Syria. Although the 280 kilometers of track between Haifa-Dera-Damascus were less than one-fifth of the total track, more than three-quarters of the passengers and freight tonnage were carried on it. Damascus was the largest market in Syria. It generated one-third of the freight and passenger receipts and was the destination for many goods and passengers embarked elsewhere. The towns of Haifa and Tiberias in Palestine were centers of the tourist trade. A large majority of the first-class round-trip tickets used on the entire line were sold there. A majority even of the third-class round-trip tickets were sold in Palestine. Medina was the only one of the seven stations having the largest passenger revenues that was not between Haifa and Damascus.

---

[29] Abdullah, *Memoirs*, pp. 120–122.

About one-half the Hijaz Railroad's stations, mostly those between Maan and Medina, had no passenger or freight income
whatsoever in 1913. Except for changes resulting from Ottoman
military control, these stations were outside the area of economic
impact. Their unproductivity resulted in losses that had to be
covered by the surplus of revenues from the northern sections of
the line. One of the few breakdowns of profits by area is for the
Haifa-Dera line in 1913, when there was a net profit of T.L.
62,824. Total profits for the whole railroad that year were only
T.L. 81,766.[30] The rest of the line. therefore, contributed less
than T.L. 20,000 in profits.

The centralization of economic activity in the Palestine region
can also be seen in an analysis of the railroad's operations in the
city of Haifa. Next to Damascus, Haifa was the chief center of
the freight and passenger business. The impact of the railroad is
more easily seen in Haifa than in Damascus because growth
there involved dramatic change. It was only with the railroad's
arrival that Haifa ceased being a very small town dependent
upon Acre. Even with the construction of the branch to Dera in
1906, trade inland continued to be hampered by the small harbor
and inadequate transfer facilities. Still the population of the
town grew. After the settlement of German religious immigrants
in the 1870s, the population was between 4,000 and 6,000. By
1914 it was about 22,000.[31] Haifa was the fastest-growing town
in Palestine.

Although the composition of Haifa's trade remained nearly the
same as it was before the coming of the railroad, the volume of
commerce was increased. The chief export was Hauran wheat.
The growth in external trade can be seen in the change between
1904, when 296,855 tons were shipped from Haifa, and 1913,
when this figure had increased to 808,763 tons.[32] Imports were
mostly European goods bound for Damascus and other towns in
the interior. One new import was coal for the Hijaz Railroad.
About 30,000 tons of it were landed in 1908.

[30] "Sikkat al-hadid al-hijaziyyah," *Al-Manar*, 25 (1924), 204–205.

[31] FRA, 3, Gaillardot (Haifa) to Bourgeois, 7 August 1906; Baedeker, *Palestine and Syria*, pp. 230 ff.

[32] "Die Hedschasbahn," p. 291.

A number of other changes took place in Haifa after the beginning of railroad construction in 1904. A school for sons of railroad officials was built, foreign post offices were opened, the consular corps was expanded, and a branch of the Imperial Ottoman Bank was constructed.[33] German influence grew with the town. In numbers and wealth Germans dominated the foreign community. Although there are no data available on income distribution in Haifa, the increase in the number of foreigners suggests that the prosperity the railroad brought may have gone in large part to foreign nationals, largely Germans.

French diplomats felt that the Ottomans were favoring Haifa at the expense of Beirut in order to decrease French influence in commerce. There is some evidence that Beirut's expansion was affected by the Hijaz Railroad. From 1911, when the Italian-Ottoman War disrupted commerce, to 1914 both imports and exports of Beirut fell by about one-quarter from their high points of 1908–10. However, in 1913 shipping tonnage in Beirut was still over twice that of Haifa.[34]

The presence of large numbers of Europeans along the Mediterranean coast led to the compilation of statistics for the commerce of the port cities. The economic life of the interior towns was not so well documented. Information concerning some stations was compiled by travelers and the Hijaz Railroad itself.

A factor that limited the railroad's capacity to effect social change was the distance between railroad stations and local settlements. Frequently railroad construction had followed the best roadbed and ignored the small villages and towns of the area. As a result stations were occasionally several kilometers distant from the nearest habitation.

Most of the small towns and villages of the interior exported more than they imported. Almost all exports were grains grown in the area around the station. In Palestine, however, there was

[33] Ibid., pp. 291–92.
[34] FRA, 321, Savoye (Damascus) to Delcassé, 1 September 1903; F.O. 195/2370, Cumberbatch (Beirut) to Lowther, 20 April 1911; al-Husni, *Tarikh*, pp. 311–12; Ottoman Empire, Administration Sanitaire, *Mouvement général et statistique comparative par pavillon de la navigation dans les ports ottomans* (Constantinople: Haim, 1914), p. 28.

a greater diversity of production. An example was the agricultural goods shipped from the village of Samakh. In 1909, 1,201 metric tons (M.T.) arrived or left Samakh by rail. Although grains were predominant with 696 M.T., there were also 167 M.T. of vegetables and 68 M.T. of fruits. In such villages and towns as Muzeirib, Busra, and Amman incoming freight was diverse, but a large majority of the freight leaving the station was grain. A third group of stations on the line between Haifa-Damascus-Maan was close to very small villages or no settled habitations at all. This group of stations included Nasib, Izra, and Deir Ali. They existed for the railroad as grain-collecting centers with almost no other freight of any sort.[35]

Another class of towns and villages affected by the railroad was the frontier settlements. As effective Ottoman political control went with the railroad into South Jordan and the Hijaz, it impinged upon a number of settlements that had previously been under other control or none at all. In certain cases the railroad, through providing physical security and economic employment, developed villages where there had been no inhabitants before.

The northernmost of the frontier settlements was Maan. It had been conquered by Ottoman troops in the 1890s. The town's 3,000 people, one third of whom were Christian, had several Ottoman elementary schools and a secondary one. The coming of the telegraph from Damascus and a larger garrison in the early 1900s caused the town to grow a little in population. New government buildings were built and Palestinian and Damascus merchants arrived. Inter- and intra-village feuding was severely limited by government garrisons.[36]

With the arrival of the Hijaz Railroad, coffee, sugar, and prepared cloth from Damascus became readily available in Maan. Although rice was still brought from Aqaba and other commodities from Palestine, most goods came by the railroad.[37] Prices

[35] *HD-7.*

[36] Cuinet, *Syrie*, pp. 505–6; Castiau, "En Syrie," pp. 58–59; *TF*, 22 Ab 1904, p. 4.

[37] Antonin Jaussen and Raphael Savignon, *Mission archéologique en Arabie (Mars-Mai 1907)* (Paris: Leroux, 1909–22), pp. 463–73.

on imported goods soon fell. Gunrunning from Aqaba and Sinai remained an important occupation for the tribes and some Ottoman officials.

In addition to the railroad's buildings, a hotel, a hospital, and a water system were constructed. The economy was boosted by an influx of tourists who traveled on the Hijaz Railroad to Maan on the way to nearby Petra. Rents for houses rose and there was greater demand for food and housing accommodations.[38]

The railroad boom that started in the early 1900s stopped with the end of construction in 1908. Many of the nearly 1,000 people who worked for the Hijaz Railroad left Maan for Damascus or Haifa. The railroad now provided goods only for the town and immediately surrounding areas rather than the larger market that had existed before 1908. Maan's initial growth turned out to be a temporary phenomenon. It became only a small railroad center and commercial distribution point.

The village of Tabuk illustrates the developmental features of the Hijaz Railroad in a more dramatic way. Late nineteenth-century travelers described Tabuk as a small village of between forty and sixty houses. Despite the presence of several sources of water the place had been deserted in 1884 because of fighting between the residents and their Rashidi overlord. The villagers who were able to take refuge in a small fortress were rescued by the pilgrimage caravan; the others were killed. By 1900 only a few of the villagers had returned. A three-way struggle between the Ottomans, the Rashidis, and the 'Atiyya, who held the area west and south of Tabuk, resulted in constant insecurity.[39]

The construction of the Hijaz Railroad brought security and economic growth to the village. Repair facilities were built at Tabuk as well as a railroad station and living quarters, water towers, and engine sheds. A sixty-bed hospital and a mosque, the latter the personal gift of Kazim Paşa, were constructed. Harb ibn Muhammad, the chief of the 'Atiyya, built a house in the village. Many of the houses near the fortress were destroyed

---

[38] Durham, "The Hedjaz Railway."

[39] H. St. J. Philby, *The Land of Midian* (London: Ernest Benn, 1957), p. 114; *TF*, 14 Nawwar 1900, p. 7; Landau, *Hejaz Railway*, p. 60.

to create a new market place; new houses were built for those evicted. The railroad dug four new wells. An Ottoman school was established and teachers were supplied. It was defended against attack. Bedouins in 1910 were defeated when they tried to raid the village. It was officially called a village by the Ottoman government in 1914 when a headman was sent from Istanbul.[40]

As long as the 'Atiyya and Rashidis remained cooperative, Ottoman control, and hence relative physical security, was maintained. Ultimately enough troops could be supplied by rail to force compliance by the tribes with Ottoman desires, at least in the immediate vicinity of the village.

Most of the changes the Hijaz Railroad caused in Syrian and Hijazi society were unplanned. The major economic change was an increase in the export of agricultural products. There was apparently a doubling of exports of Hauran wheat to Haifa between 1903 and 1910. Wheat that had been processed was also shipped in bulk on the railroad. Flour milled in Damascus was sent to Haifa. Between 1903 and 1912 grain averaged slightly less than one-half of total freight. The railroad encouraged producers to send wheat to Haifa; it cost five-sixths less to ship wheat by rail than by camel.[41]

The railroad itself engaged in only one attempt at economic development. Blanckenhorn, a German explorer, was sent in 1905 to look for phosphates near Salt. Although deposits were found, concessions granted, and a spur line planned, no mining was done because the phosphates had too little commercial value. The Hijaz Railroad also supported the establishment of a series of stores, hotels, and inns from Damascus to al-Ula. Twice a month special wagons for those living in the settlements in the

---

[40] Hamilton, *Problems of the Middle East*, p. 284; *TF*, 10 Aylul 1906, p. 2; 26 Ab 1907, p. 4; Durham, "The Hedjaz Railway"; Philby, *Midian*, p. 122; F.O. 195/2277, Devey (Damascus) to Barclay, 2 July 1908; Musil, *Northern Hegaz*, p. 234.
[41] Al-Husni, *Tarikh*, pp. 239–40, 281; Cuinet, *Syrie*, p. 439; a similar growth in production took place in Anatolia following the construction of new railroad lines, but camel transport remained competitive with railroads there for a much longer time than in Syria (Quataert, "Ottoman Reform," p. 208).

desert were attached to trains going to Medina. Vegetables and
fruits were sold on credit at Damascus prices set by the railroad.[42] The railroad was used by the Ottoman post to ship mail;
postal offices were built at some of the stations. Although the
Hijaz Railroad's telegraph was used primarily by the railroad
and other governmental agencies, it was available for private use
also.

International Quarantine Controls and Ottoman Autonomy

The Hijaz Railroad transported pilgrims to Medina faster than
had been possible by camel caravan. The increased speed made
the danger of communicating disease greater. Before 1900 Europeans depended upon the quarantine stations they controlled at
Tur in Sinai and Kamaran Island in the Red Sea to stop diseases
from spreading from the Hijaz. The overland route from Medina
had not been regulated. Disease prevention in the Hijaz itself
was nearly unknown. In the 1890s alone there had been four
major occurrences of cholera, with thousands of deaths.[43] There
were few doctors in Mecca and Medina.

In view of the apparent Ottoman inability to improve health
in the Hijaz, the European states assumed control of Ottoman
quarantine stations through the international Health Council of
Constantinople. Ottoman attempts to resist growing European
control of the quarantine were futile. They were able only to
block the changes they opposed in the treaties governing international health.[44]

The Ottoman government set up a quarantine service for the
Hijaz Railroad pilgrims. A nominal quarantine had been supposed to take place for the camel caravans at Zarqa. The duration of the quarantine was extended to ten days and its site was

---

[42] Durham, "The Hedjaz Railway"; Musil, *Northern Hegaz*, p. 161; Interview with Hasan Nas'a, 13 January 1970.

[43] Ahmed Chérif, *Le pèlerinage de la Mecque* (Beirut: Angelil, 1930), p. 61; C.
Stékoulis, *Le pèlerinage de la Mecque et le choléra au Hedjaz* (Constantinople: De
Castro, 1883), pp. 13–24; Kasim Izzettin, *Hicaz'da Teşkilat ve Islahat-i Sıhhiye ve
1329 Senesi Hacc-i Şerif* (Istanbul: Matbaa-i amire, 1328/1910), pp. 5–8.

[44] Young, *Corps*, III, 126–27, 130–34, 168–74.

moved to Maan in 1902. The temporary facilities were improved only in 1908–9 when a regular lazaret was established at Tabuk. The lazaret was financed by a special tax of twenty-five kuruş on pilgrims' railroad tickets. It was built to hold 4,000 pilgrims at one time. The railroad arranged to ship pilgrims to Tabuk in groups small enough to avoid overtaxing the lazaret's capacity. The pilgrims and their goods as well as the coaches and personnel of the railroad were disinfected there. The railroad had to have special crews to operate between Medina and Tabuk; they could go north of Tabuk only after going through quarantine.[45]

The European states refused to accept an Ottoman-controlled quarantine as safe. They insisted that pilgrims use either Kamaran or Tur. Some Egyptian pilgrims used the Hijaz Railroad despite this. If they were found to have done so, the Egyptian government compelled them to go from their port of entry on the Mediterranean to the Tur lazaret before entering Egypt.[46] France also tried to forbid pilgrims from North Africa the use of the railroad. Apparently attempts were made to discourage pilgrims from using the railroad up to the outbreak of World War I.

Competition with the French

Relations between the Hijaz Railroad and its chief competitor, the Damas, Hama et Prolongements Railroad, had been strained from the very inception of the Damascus-Medina line in 1900. From the point of view of the French company the government-operated Hijaz Railroad posed unfair competition. At the very time when the D.H.P. was beginning to make a profit after years of financial losses, the Hijaz Railroad added new competition. Since the Hijaz line did not have to make a profit, had no debt, and was backed by the Imperial Treasury, it seemed impossible to compete with it. The Damascus-Dera part of the Hijaz sys-

[45] Rifaat, *Rapport général* pp. 10–17 and 19–23; Gabriel Delamare, *La défense sanitaire de la ligne Médine-Damas* (Constantinople: L. Mourkidès, 1912), pp. 5–6, 15; *TF*, 3 Shubat 1908, p. 5; 17 Shubat 19, p. 5.

[46] F.O. 368/180, Morrison (Alexandria) to Gould, 24 March 1908; F.O. 368/228, Clemow (Constantinople) to O'Conor, 31 January 1908; *TF*, 19 T al-A 1908, p. 4.

tem, close to and parallel with the Damascus-Muzeirib branch of the D.H.P., ruined the French line's Damascus-Beirut wheat exports. Since Haifa-Dara was not so affected by heavy winter snows or the steep gradients that made the Lebanese route expensive, it seemed sure that shippers would eventually switch to the Hijaz Railroad. The Ottoman railroad also precluded the possibility of major expansion south into Palestine. The French were hemmed in between the German-controlled Baghdad Railroad in the north and the Ottoman Hijaz Railroad in the south.

This picture of unrelieved gloom needs to be considered in the light of a number of developments favorable to the French. An agreement of 18 May 1905 between the Ottomans and the D.H.P. compensated the latter for possible losses on the Damascus-Muzeirib line with a lump-sum payment of T.L. 150,000. The D.H.P.'s profits on its operations rose in the following years up to 1914 and the value of the railroad's stock increased.[47] Most important was the construction of new lines joining Riyaq with Aleppo and Homs with Tripoli. The broad-gauge Riyaq-Aleppo line with a subsidy guaranteed by the Ottomans was especially profitable. The D.H.P.'s extension north of Hama was granted by the Ottomans as part of the package compromise of 1905. It was part of the compensation for alleged unfair competition caused by construction of parallel lines. While the receipts from the Damascus-Muzeirib section of the D.H.P. declined from about T.L. 27,200 in 1908 to T.L. 16,800 in 1912, they rose on the Damascus-Beirut line and increased dramatically on the newer sections of the system as they came into operation.[48] The reasons for the D.H.P. attack on the Hijaz Railroad were not immediate financial problems. The D.H.P. feared that the Hijaz Railroad would become a greater competitor in the future; the French line desired to achieve a monopoly of railroad transport in Syria.

Negotiations in Paris between the French and Ottoman governments, which began in 1912, resulted in two agreements con-

---

[47] Eleftériadès, *Les chemins de fer*, p. 116; for the text of the 1905 agreement, see pp. 63–64.

[48] FRA, 329, D.H.P. to Ministry, 25 April 1913.

cerning the Hijaz Railroad. Bargaining involved a number of factors other than the railroad. Chief of these was the pressing need
of the Ottomans for large amounts of money that could be raised
only on the Paris Bourse. The approval of the French government was also needed for an increase in the Ottoman customs
rates. The French Foreign Ministry granted permission to float
Ottoman loans in Paris. In return the Ottomans made a number
of economic concessions. Although the D.H.P. had expressly
stated in the Agreement of 1905 that it would seek no further
compensation for losses caused by the Hijaz Railroad's competition, it nevertheless submitted a series of proposals that were
substantially incorporated by the French into their bargaining
terms.

The military disasters of the Italian and Balkan wars caused
the Ottomans to agree to the French terms. Strengthening the
Ottoman Empire's armies to defend its capital was more important than the Hijaz Railroad. The agreement of 11 September
1913 between France and the Ottoman Empire, insofar as it
dealt with Syria, called for the concession of a new railroad from
Riyaq to Ramla to be built by the D.H.P.[49] This line would link
the Beirut-Damascus D.H.P. with the Jaffa-Jerusalem Railroad
and parallel the Hijaz Railroad's Damascus-Dera-Maan section.
Its construction would have diverted most of Palestine's commerce away from the Hijaz Railroad. A direct blow to the autonomy of the Hijaz Railroad was the provision that a Frenchman
who had been a director of a French railroad would be appointed
for a ten-year period as the Hijaz Railroad's director. His powers
were to be specified in detail. The rates charged by the D.H.P.
and Hijaz Railroad were to be adjusted so as to lessen competition between them. The port facilities of Tripoli, Jaffa, and
Haifa were to be entrusted to French companies. If the Damas-
cus-Maan part of the Hijaz Railroad were ever to be leased, it
had to be to the D.H.P.

Because the Ottoman Cabinet balked at certain sections of the
agreement and the French desired to include new provisions, the
document never came into force. Instead, a new agreement was

---

[49] For the text, see FRA, 330, 1 September 1913.

signed on 9 April 1914 and approved by the Ottomans on 22 April 1914. New clauses in addition to the 1913 text stopped the Afula-Nablus branch of the Hijaz Railroad from being extended toward Jerusalem. There was to be a guaranteed increase of 5 percent per year in the revenues of the D.H.P.'s Damascus-Muzeirib line over its 1913 income. In Annex 5 the Ottoman government declared that "because of the special character" of the Hijaz Railroad it could not be yielded to a concessionnaire, but at the same time it promised that the effective administration of the Damascus-Dera-Haifa part of the railroad would be under French control.[50]

This agreement was not put into force because of the advent of World War I. Ironically, precisely the reverse occurred, for on 3 November 1914 the D.H.P. was seized as enemy property. Its administration was awarded to the Hijaz Railroad for the duration of the War.

World War I: Military Capacity under Stress

When the Ottoman Empire entered the war on the side of Germany in November 1914, it faced invasions and major attacks on a number of fronts. There was heavy fighting in the Caucasus against the Russians, in Iraq against the British, at the Dardanelles leading to the capital of Istanbul itself against a joint Allied army. One of the few places where the Ottomans felt they could take the offensive was in South Syria, from which they hoped to launch an invasion of Egypt. Their chief purpose was to disrupt and perhaps close the Suez Canal.

To accomplish the invasion of Egypt, the Ottomans took a number of steps designed to improve transportation in the region. The Ottomans were dependent upon their ability to transport and equip large numbers of troops in arid lands far from bases of supply. The Hijaz Railroad became a key element in the first years of the war.

The second major phase of World War I in the Arab lands of

[50] FRA, 331, D.H.P. to Director of Political and Commercial Affairs, Ministry of Foreign Affairs, 17 October 1913; FRA, 332, Bompard (Constantinople) to Ministry, 22 April 1914.

the Ottoman Empire began in 1916 with the revolt of the Amir Husayn of the Hijaz against the central government. With the help of the British, Husayn announced the independence of the Hijaz in particular and the Arab people in general. For religious prestige it was necessary for the Ottomans to retain as much control in the Hijaz as possible. After the loss of Mecca, Jidda, and Taif to Husayn at the beginning of the revolt, the Ottomans held only Medina, the southern terminus of the Hijaz Railroad. The defense of Medina, the control of the routes leading to it, and the defense of South Syria against the Arab army led by Husayn's son Faysal all depended upon the successful utilization of the railroad.

Abdülhamid's desire for an inland railroad to link the major cities of the Ottoman-Arab area was justified by the events of the war. British control of the Mediterranean and Red seas did not disrupt the Hijaz Railroad because the track was beyond the reach of naval guns. Instead, the railroad's problems resulted largely from the incomplete state of the Baghdad Railroad. Supplies from Germany and Anatolia could not be transported to the Hijaz Railroad easily. The chief accomplishment of the railroad was to supply and transport large numbers of troops in Palestine and the Hijaz. Completion of the Palestinian sections of the Hijaz Railroad received high priority. They were a prerequisite to a successful large-scale invasion of Sinai.

In the years immediately before the war began, extensions south to Nablus and Jerusalem had been added to the Haifa-Dera branch of the Hijaz Railroad. Between 1915 and 1918 this program was expanded. About T.L. 600,000 was budgeted for construction of the new track. The former head of construction, Meissner Paşa, was recalled in October 1915 from the Baghdad Railroad to supervise Palestinian operations. By the time of his arrival the railroad had reached Beersheba.[51] Sixty-two kilometers were added to the railroad by the summer of 1916.

Since new railroad matériel from Europe was not available in large quantities during the war, the equipment belonging to

[51] Eleftériadès, *Les chemins de fer*, p. 176; George F. McMunn and Cyril Falls, *Military Operations* (London: H.M.S.O., 1928), pp. 85–86.

other lines was used. The D.H.P.'s Damascus-Muzeirib and
Tripoli-Homs tracks were taken up. The Jaffa-Ramla section of
the Jaffa-Jerusalem Railroad was destroyed and the rails used for
the Hijaz Railroad. The railroad's own branches from Dera to
Busra and Haifa to Acre were similarly demolished for the Palestinian extensions.[52]

Two new Hijaz Railroad branches were built during World
War I. The first was a spur line from the station just outside the
walls of Medina to the citadel inside the city. A forty-kilometer
line between Unayza and Shaubak in Jordan was built in 1916.
It was designed to transport wood cut in forests there to the main
line for use as fuel. Since coal imports were stopped by the British blockade of the Mediterranean, engines had to use wood as
fuel. Thousands of trees in the Ajlun, Salt, and Yarmuk areas
were cut down.[53]

The effect of the construction and supply problems was to
hamper the Ottoman invasion of Egypt, which reached the Suez
Canal but had to retreat. Ottoman supply lines depended upon
camel transport across the Sinai Peninsula back to the rail terminus. A large army could not be maintained in the field without greater quantities of matériel, especially water, than the
camel caravans provided. Over 120 trains of 13 wagons each
were used for transporting troops to the railroad's terminus.[54]
The British and Allied armies eventually attacked the Ottoman
armies located in southern Palestine and faced the same problems of supply. Once the Allies reached Gaza, the ensuing battles with the Ottomans involved hundreds of thousands of troops
in what was for several years a nearly static front.

The right wing of the Allied armies in Syria was held by the
Arab army, which had moved north from the Hijaz. Despite a
number of raids and a protracted siege by the Arabs, Medina's
Ottoman garrison still held out. On the other hand, the Otto-
mans were unable to venture successfully far beyond Medina.
Ottoman control of Medina depended upon supplies coming

[52] Peake, *History of Jordan*, p. 97; al-Marawani, *Al-Khatt*, pp. 35–36.
[53] Madi and Musa, *Tarikh al-Urdunn*, p. 30.
[54] Al-Marawani, *Al-Khatt*, p. 36.

over the Hijaz Railroad. Unable to defeat the Medina garrison, the Arab army and its British advisers adopted a policy of attrition.[55] In Palestine the Hijaz Railroad, the chief method of supply for the Ottoman armies, was relatively safe from attack. In the Hijaz and South Jordan it became the chief battlefield.

The Arab army launched a series of attacks against the railroad. At the beginning of hostilities in 1916 an average of two trains per day went from Damascus to Medina. The raids by the Arab forces soon forced the Ottomans to send only two per week.[56] The first major interruption in service took place in March 1917. As a result regular patrols between stations were established, the defenses of the southern stations were strengthened, and reinforcements were sent to the area where the raids had occurred.

The Arab forces were fighting over 25,000 Ottoman troops south of Amman. It soon became apparent that the Arab forces could not successfully attack Ottoman regulars in fixed positions.[57] However, as the Arabs gained experience, their raids began to interfere with the operation of the line. All passenger service was suspended on 2 January 1917 for the duration of the war.

The damage the Arab forces inflicted on the railroad was repaired in many cases. Track repairs could be made at the rate of one kilometer of double track per day. Although the number of bridges and culverts destroyed and of tracks uprooted increased steadily in 1917, the damage could still be overcome by temporary repairs. Broken rails were repaired at Madain Salih. There were large reserves of rails in Medina that had been stored there before the war in preparation for the planned expansion south to Mecca. Spare parts were not so easily available. The deteriora-

[55] T. E. Lawrence, *Seven Pillars of Wisdom* (Garden City, N.Y.: Doubleday, 1935), pp. 134–35; Suleiman Mousa, *T. E. Lawrence* (London: Oxford Univ. Press, 1966), p. 122.

[56] *AB*, no. 37, 4 January 1917, p. 4; *AB*, no. 42, 15 February 1917, p. 74.

[57] *AB*, No. 43, 28 February 1917, p. 97; *AB*, No. 46, 30 March 1917, pp. 144–45; McMunn and Falls, *Military* (1928), p. 237; George F. McMunn and Cyril Falls, *Military Operations* (London: H.M.S.O., 1930), Part II, p. 409; *AB* no. 52, 31 May 1917, p. 249; *AB*, no. 42, 15 February 1917, p. 84.

tion in rolling stock decreased the speed at which trains could travel.[58]

Starting in late October 1917, whole trains were captured. Then intermediate posts on the railroad began to fall. Finally, long-term interruptions in the northern Hijaz sections were obtained by Arab action. By February 1918 traffic from Damascus to Medina was almost completely stopped; the last through train was in April.[59] The key tunnels and the Yarmuk bridges of the railroad were taken by the Allies in the spring of 1918. However, the southern part of the line remained in Ottoman control.

With the cutting of the line south of Maan two separate areas of battle were created. In the north the fuel situation became crucial after the Arab forces began to raid the chief sources of wood in September 1917. The use of Lebanese coal had been abandoned earlier because it was too full of brimstone. It was discovered that the wood that was substituted for coal caused fires on the trains. It also provided less energy than coal. Despite the fuel problems operations continued until enemy action stopped traffic. Amman and Qatrana stations were bombed from the air in June 1918 after both had been raided. The capture of Muzeirib and destruction around Dera slowed the retreat of the Ottoman army in Palestine and contributed greatly to its casualties after the main front was broken in 1918. The fall of Damascus in 1 October 1918 was followed by the abolition of the Ottoman Hijaz Railroad operations administration and the creation of an Arab General Directorate for the railroad.[60]

On the southern part of the line fighting continued for a longer period of time. The commander of the garrison of Medina had supplied fuel for the railroad by destroying many of the city's houses. Stockpiles of war matériel were built up before the railroad was cut. The treasures of the Prophet's mosque were removed before the last train left. After 12 October 1918, when the Arab army took Tabuk, only the city of Medina continued

[58] *AB*, no. 84, 7 April 1918, pp. 111–12.

[59] *AB*, no. 80, 26 February 1918, pp. 57–60; *AB*, no. 92, 11 June 1918, pp. 185–86.

[60] *AB*, no. 93, 18 June 1918, pp. 205–206; *AB*, no. 104, 24 September 1918, p. 332; al-Marawani, *Al-Khatt*, p. 6.

to hold out. Even after the armistice between the Ottoman Empire and the Allies was signed, Medina defied orders from Istanbul to surrender. The city was yielded only on 10 January 1919.[61] Ottoman control of the Hijaz Railroad came completely to an end with the fall of the empire in the Arab lands.

[61] Elie Kedourie, "The Surrender of Medina," *Middle Eastern Studies*, 13 (1977), 124–43.

Distinguished pilgrims in front of the engine that is to draw their train to Medina

Pilgrims returning from the Hijaz

Returning pilgrims

Returning pilgrims

The dangers of rock slippage during operations

Conclusions

THE EXPANSION OF Europe in the late nineteenth and early twentieth centuries touched all parts of the world. Conclusions drawn from the Ottoman attempt to meet this expansion as seen in the Hijaz Railroad project may illuminate similar processes that took place elsewhere at that time. Ottoman experience in attempting to increase military capacity while retaining political autonomy involved the same considerations that affected other societies concerned with selective cultural and technological borrowing from Europe.

Direct military danger from European expansion was not the only reason Sultan Abdülhamid II ordered the construction of the Hijaz Railroad. The sultan wished to extend Ottoman central political authority to the Hijaz and South Syria for the first time in effective form. He saw European influence, particularly that of France in Syria and Britain in the Arabian Peninsula, as the chief danger to this centralization.[1] The Hijaz Railroad was

---

[1] Sultan Abdülhamid II said in 1906, "Our Mecca Railroad proves that we

the method chosen to enforce centralization; with it local military superiority could be acquired.

Europeans had succeeded in gaining control of much of the economic life along the coasts of Syria. Opposition to Ottoman reform was weaker inland. Interference by Europeans in the railroad was made difficult when it was termed a holy railroad, dedicated to the pilgrimage to Mecca. The Hijaz was effectively outside the reach both of European influence and the control of the Ottoman central government.

The building and financing of the railroad show a blending of old and new ideas and values. The Pan-Islamic idea of the caliph as defender of the faith and community was used to raise funds for technical innovation. Success in construction and operation was seen as added proof that the Ottoman state was acting on behalf of all Muslims as guardian of the Holy Places of Islam.

Ottoman attempts to build their own state railroads had in the past been failures. Initial plans to use only Ottoman matériel and technical personnel in the Hijaz Railroad's construction were unsuccessful. Foreign help was necessary. German engineers dominated significant parts of the line's administration during construction. On the other hand, Ottoman soldiers provided the labor to build most of the line. In order to get the railroad built rapidly, the goal of Ottoman independence of Westerners had to be compromised.

In the short time between 1908 and 1918 some successes were achieved in administration of operations. Ottoman personnel were trained for some technical posts. Most upper administrative and skilled labor positions remained in the hands of foreigners. This was of relatively little importance as long as ultimate administrative control remained with the central government. The main goal of the railroad was achieved when the military opera-

---

are capable of progress, that we can hold back even England herself. What hasn't she tried in order to cause our railroad to Mecca to fail!" (Ali Vahbi Bey, *Avant la débacle*, p. 91); Engin Deniz Akarli, "The Problems of External Pressures, Power Struggles, and Budgetary Deficits in Ottoman Politics under Abdülhamid II (1876–1909)," Diss., Princeton Univ., 1976, repeatedly cites instances of Abdülhamid's suspicion of and enmity toward Britain.

tions of 1908–10 and 1914–18 demonstrated the railroad's usefulness in transporting troops and munitions.

The economic success of the railroad's operations and its rapid and cheap construction stand in sharp contrast to other Ottoman steps toward independent economic development. The corruption, inefficiency, and torpor of other Ottoman state enterprises were noticeably absent from the Hijaz Railroad. Careful attention by the chief political figures at the Court in Istanbul accounts for the success enjoyed in the period 1902–8. At least as important, the supply of money was scarcely ever interrupted. Unlike foreign concessions, the Hijaz Railroad at least covered its own operating expenses.

Despite the absence of previous railroad experience among Ottoman administrators, successful passenger, freight, and operations departments were created. These were largely the result of the work of Germans serving in the operations administration. On the other hand, Ottomans were responsible for the expansion of the railroad in southern Syria. Construction of branches between 1910 and 1914 brought new areas under control for the first time. The urgency of political centralization to the leaders of the empire was made clear by their expenditure of funds for this purpose during a period of war and internal political strife. Railroad transport of troops meant that punitive expeditions could be moved cheaply enough that their cost approximated the gains which resulted to the empire from their success.

The sections of the Hijaz Railroad in Palestine were essential to the line's military effectiveness and economic viability. During World War I the Hijaz Railroad in Palestine brought troops and supplies to the borders of Sinai. Large British and Allied forces were resisted successfully until 1918. The economic impact of the railroad was felt most strongly in Haifa. It became a major outlet for South Syrian wheat and the entry point for imports to the interior.

Enterprises such as the Hijaz Railroad are not susceptible to analysis based solely on financial calculations. As with other manifestations of state socialism, the railroad involved considerations of national security and prestige that cannot be measured by profit and loss. An example is the issue of gaining military control of the Hijaz. The Hijaz was not desired because of any taxes it might yield the empire, for the Hijaz Vilayet was revenue absorbing rather than producing. The Hijaz was valuable because control and protection of the Holy Places gave increased status to the rulers of the Ottoman Empire.

By 1914 that empire was on the verge of surrendering control over the most important sections of the Hijaz Railroad to a French-owned railroad company. The independence and effectiveness of the railroad would have been ended. Although temporarily saved by World War I, the defeat of the Ottoman Army at the end of the war placed the railroad under foreign control at last. An experiment in increasing Ottoman political and military capacity was ended as the empire itself approached dissolution and radical transformation into the successor nation states of the modern Middle East.

APPENDIX

SELECTED BIBLIOGRAPHY

INDEX

APPENDIX

Principal Stations of the Hijaz Railroad in 1914

Names of stations	Distance from Damascus in kilometers
Damascus	0
Kiswe	21
Deir Ali	31
Masjid	50
Jebab	63
Khabab	69
Muhajjah	78
Shaqra	85
Izra	91
Dera	123
Nasib	136
Mafraq	162
Samra	185
Zarqa	203
Amman	222
Jiza	260
Qatrana	326
Maan	459
Ghadir al-Hajj	475
Batn al-Ghul	520
Mudawwara	572
Tabuk	692
Al-Akhdar	760
Al-Muazzam	822
Ad-Dar al-Hamra	880
Madain Salih	955
Al-Ula	980
Hadiyya	1,133
Medina	1,302

	Distance from Haifa
Haifa	0
Afula	37
Bisan	60
Jisr al-Majami	77
Samakh	87
Muzeirib	150
Dera	162

SELECTED BIBLIOGRAPHY

Unpublished Material

Durham, University of. School of Oriental Studies. Sudan Archives, "Reports and papers relating to the Hijaz Railway including a secret report by H. Channer, June 1909 (5 pp.) 1906–1909."

France. Ministère des Affaires Étrangères. Turquie. Chemins de fer: Réseau Asiatique, 1898–1918.

————. Indes. Politique intérieure. Question Musulman—Panislamisme, 1906–1917.

————. Turquie. Politique intérieure: Arabie—Yemen, 1896–1914.

————. Turquie. Politique intérieure: Arabie—Yemen, Pèlerinage de la Mecque, 1896–1917.

————. Turquie. Politique intérieure: Palestine, 1898–1914.

————. Turquie. Politique intérieure: Syrie, Liban, 1899–1914.

Great Britain. Foreign Office 78/5452, The Hijaz Railway, 1900–1905.

————. F.O. 78/5451, Haifa-Damascus Railroad, 1902–1905.

————. F.O. 195, Consular reports from Beirut, Haifa, Damascus, and Jidda, 1900–1911.

————. F.O. 368, Commercial, 1906–1920.

————. F.O. 371, Political (Constantinople Embassy, 1900–1914).

————. F.O. 618/3, Consular reports from Damascus, 1900–1914.

————. F.O. 882/25–28, *The Arab Bulletin*.

India Office Archives (London). Political and Secret Department. L/P and S. 10/12: 3142/1903 "Arabia: The Hedjaz Railway, 1901–1912" and associated papers.

Turkey. Başbakanlık Arşivi. Yıldız Collection. 36. 140/66. 140. XXIII. Hicaz Demiryolu için toplanan ianelerin kaydına mahsus defter (9 Temmuz 1318–16 Haziran 1319/1902–1903).

Personal interviews with Hasan Nas'a, 13 January 1970, in Amman; Muhammad Nadim al-Sawwaf, 20 November 1969, in Damascus; Mrs. Ahmad Tuqan, 18 January 1970, in Amman; Shaykh Turki, 24 January 1970, in Amman.

Printed Sources

Abdullah, King of Transjordan. *Memoirs of King Abdullah of Transjordan*. London: Jonathan Cape, 1950.

Abu Manneh, Butros. "Sultan Abdülhamid II and the Sharifs of Mecca (1880–1900)." *Asian and African Studies*, 9 (1973), 1–21.

Ahmad, Aziz. *Studies in Islamic Culture in the Indian Environment.* Oxford: Clarendon Press, 1964.

Ahmad, Feroz. *The Young Turks: The Committee of Union and Progress in Turkish Politics, 1908–1914.* Oxford: Oxford Univ. Press, 1969.

Akarli, Engin Deniz. "The Problems of External Pressures, Power Struggles, and Budgetary Deficits in Ottoman Politics under Abdülhamid II (1876–1909): Origins and Solutions." Diss., Princeton, 1976.

Ali Vahbi Bey, comp. *Avant la débacle de la Turquie: Pensées et souvenirs de l'ex Sultan Abdul-Hamid, recuellis par Ali Vahbi Bey.* Paris: Attinger frères, 1922.

Al-Amr, Saleh Muhammad. "The Hijaz under Ottoman Rule, 1869–1914: The Ottoman Vali, the Sharif of Mecca, and the Growth of British Influence." Diss., Univ. of Leeds, 1974.

Auler, Karl. *Die Hedschasbahn.* Gotha: J. Perthes, 1906.

ʾAwad, ʾAbd al-ʾAziz. *Al-Idarat al-ʾUthmaniyyah fi wilayah Suriya, 1864–1914.* Cairo: Dar al-Maʾarif, 1969.

Baedeker, Karl, comp. *Palestine and Syria.* 5th ed. Leipzig: Baedeker, 1912.

Barru, Tawfiq ʾAli. *Al-ʾArab wa al-Turk fi al-ʾahd al-dusturi al-ʾuthmani, 1908–1914.* Cairo: The Arab League. Institute of Higher Arab Studies, 1960.

Al-Batanuni, Muhammad. *Al-Rihlat al-hijaziyyah li wali al-ʾniam al-hajj ʾAbbas Hilmi Basha al-Thani Kadiw Misr.* 2d. ed. Cairo: Matbaʾat al-Jamaliyyah, 1329/1911.

Bayhum, Muhammad. *Kawafil al-ʾurubah wa ma wakabaha khilal al-ʾusur.* 2 vols. Beirut: Matbaʾat al-Kashf, 1948–1950.

Bell, Gertrude L. *The Desert and the Sown.* London: Heinemann, 1907.

———. "Turkish Rule East of Jordan." *Nineteenth Century,* 52 (1902), 226–38.

Bérard, Victor. "L'incident de Tabah." *Revue de Paris,* 13 (1906), 206–24.

———. *Le sultan, l'Islam et les puissances: Constantinople– La Mecque–Bagdad.* Paris: A. Colin, 1907.

Bidwell. R., ed. *Correspondence respecting the Affairs of Arabia, 1905–1906.* London: Cass, 1971.

Bigham, Clive, Viscount Mersey. *With the Turkish Army in Thessaly.* London: Macmillan, 1897.

Blaisdell, Donald C. *European Financial Control in the Ottoman Empire.* New York: Columbia Univ. Press, 1929.

Blanckenhorn, M. "Die Hedschaz-Bahn auf Grund eigener Reisestudien." *Zeitschrift der Gesellschaft für Erdkundes zu Berlin* (1907), pp. 218–45, 288–320.

Bliss, W. Tyler. "The Sultan's Dummy Railway." *Harper's Weekly,* 50 (1906), 733–36.

Borel, Eugène. *Répartition des annuités de la dette publique ottomane: sentence arbitrale.* Geneva: A. Kundig, 1925.

C.E.B. "Notes sur le Panislamisme." *Questions Diplomatiques et Coloniales*, 28 (1909), 641–56, 729–42.

Carpenter, Frank G. *The Holy Land and Syria.* Garden City, N.Y.: Doubleday, Page and Co., 1922.

Carruthers, Douglas. *Arabian Adventure: To the Great Nefud in Quest of the Oryx.* London: Witherby, 1935.

Castiau, Marcel. "En Syrie: le long du chemin des pèlerins de la Mecque." *Bulletin de la Société Royale de Géographie d'Anvers*, 27 (1903), 19–65.

Charmes, Gabriel. *L'Avenir de la Turquie: le Panislamisme.* Paris: Calman-Levy, 1883.

Chérif, Ahmed. *Le pèlerinage de la Mecque.* Beirut: Angelil, 1930.

Chevallier, Dominique. "À Damas, production et société à la fin du XIXe siècle." *Annales Economies-Sociétés-Civilisation*, 19 (1964), 966–72.

———. "Un exemple de résistance technique de l'artisanat syrien aux XIXe et XXe siècles." *Syria*, 30 (1962), 300–324.

Courau, J. *La Locomotive en Turquie d'Asie.* Brussels: Guyot, 1895.

Cuinet, Vital. *Syrie, Liban et Palestine: géographie administrative.* Paris: Leroux, 1896.

Davison, Roderic. "Nationalism as an Ottoman Problem and the Ottoman Response." In William Haddad and William Ochsenwald, eds., *Nationalism in a Non-National State: The Dissolution of the Ottoman Empire.* Columbus: Ohio State Univ. Press, 1977, pp. 25–56.

Dawn, C. Earnest. *From Ottomanism to Arabism.* Urbana: Univ. of Illinois Press, 1973.

Delamare, Gabriel. *La défense sanitaire de la ligne Médine-Damas.* Constantinople: L. Mourkidès, 1912.

De Tarrazi, Philippe. *Tarikh al-sihafat al-ʾarabiyyah.* Beirut: Al-Matbaʾat al-Adabiyyah, 1913–1933.

Dieckmann, Peter. "Die Zweiglinie Affula-Jerusalem." *Zeitschrift des Deutscher Palästina-Vereins*, 37 (1914), 267–70.

Dominian, L. "Railroads of Turkey." *American Geographical Society of New York Bulletin*, 47 (1915), 934–40.

Dussaud, René, and Frédéric Macler. *Mission dans les régions désertiques de la Syrie Moyenne.* Paris: Imprimerie Nationale, 1903.

Düstur. 3d series, 7 vols. Istanbul: N.p., 1911–1917.

Eleftériadès, Eleuthère. *Les chemins de fer en Syrie et au Liban.* Beirut: Imprimerie Catholique, 1944.

Erişçi, Lütfü. *Türkiye'de Işçi Sınıfının Tarihi.* Istanbul: Kutulmaş Basımevi, 1951.

Erkin, Osman. "Hicaz Demiryolu." *Demiryollar Dergisi*, 22 (1948), 21–25.

Feis, Herbert. *Europe, the World's Banker, 1871–1914*. New Haven: Yale Univ. Press, 1930.

Fesch, Paul. *Constantinople aux derniers jours d'Abdul-Hamid*. Paris: Marcel Rivière, 1907.

Goodrich-Freer, A. *In a Syrian Saddle*. London: Methuen, 1905.

Great Britain. Admiralty. Naval Intelligence Division. *A Handbook of Arabia*. London: H.M.S.O., 1916.

———. Parliament. *Parliamentary Papers* (Accounts and Papers), 87, (1911) Cmd. 5707.

———. Parliament. *Parliamentary Papers* (Accounts and Papers), 116, (1908) Cmd. 3727.

Griffiths, Merwin A. "The Reorganization of the Ottoman Army under Abdülhamid II, 1880–1897." Diss., Univ. of California, Los Angeles, 1966.

Gubser, Peter A. *Politics and Change in al-Karak, Jordan*. London: Oxford Univ. Press, 1973.

Guine, Antoine, ed. *Les Communications en Syrie*. Damascus: Office Arabe de presse et de documentation, 1968.

Guthe, Hermann. "Die Hedschasbahn von Damaskus nach Medina: Ihr Bau und ihre Bedeutung." *Länder und Volker der Türkei*, 7 (1917).

Hafiz, 'Ali. *Fusul min tarikh al-Madinat al-Munawwarah*. Jidda: Shirkat al-Madinat al-Munawwarah li al-Tiba'a, n.d.

Hamilton, Angus. *Problems of the Middle East*. London: Nash, 1909.

———. *Twenty Years in Baghdad and Syria*. London: Simpkin and Marshall, 1916.

Harran, Ahmed Mohammed. "Turkish-Syrian Relations in the Ottoman Constitutional Period (1908–1914)." Diss., London, 1969.

Hecker, M. "Die Eisenbahnen der asiatischen Türkei." *Archiv für Eisenbahnwesen*, 27 (1914), 744–800, 1057–87, 1283–1321.

"Die Hedschasbahn." *Archiv für Eisenbahnwesen*, 39 (1916), 289–315.

[Hijaz Railroad]. *Hicaz Demiryolu Layihası*. Istanbul: N.p., 1324/1906–7.

———. *Hicaz Demiryolunun 1324 Senesi Varidat ve Masarifatına . . . Hesabiye*. Istanbul: N.p., [1909?].

———. *Hicaz Demiryolunun 1327 Senesi Istatistik Rapor*. Istanbul: Arşak Aruvyan Matbaası, 1328/1910.

———. *Hicaz Demiryolunun Varidat ve Masarif-i ve Terakki-i Inşaatı ile Hattın Ahvalı Umumiyesi Hakkında Malumat-i Ihsaiye ve Izahat-i Lazimegi Muhtevidir, 1330*. Istanbul: Evkaf-i Islamiye Matbaası, 1334/1915–1916.

———. *Hicaz Demiryolu Hareket Nizamnamesi*. Istanbul: Arşak Aruvyan Matbaası, 1327/1909–1910.

———. *Hicaz ve askeri demiryollar ve limanlar idare-i umumiyesi . . . talimatname*. Istanbul: N.p., 1333/1914–1915.

————. *Hicaz ve Süriye Hututı Memurin ve Müstahdeminin Sınıf ve Dere-celerine Maaşlar Cedvel*. Istanbul: N.p., n.d.

Holman, James K. "Sacred Line to Madina: The History of the Hejaz Railway." A.B. Thesis, Princeton, 1967.

Al-Husni, ʾAli. *Tarikh Suriya al-iqtisadi*. Damascus: Matbaʾah Badaiʾ al-Funun, 1342/1923–1924.

Ibrahim Rifʾat Paşa. *Mirat al-haramayn*. 2 vols. Cairo: Matbaʾah Dar al-Kutub al-Misriyyah, 1344/1925–1926.

Insha Allah, Muhammad. *The History of the Hamidia Hedjaz Railway Project*. Lahore: Central Printing Works, n.d.

International Resources Engineering and Exploration Group. The Executive Committee for the Recommissioning of the Hedjaz Railway Line. *Design Report*. New York: N.p., 1957.

"Istanbul'dan Medine'ye." *Hayat* (Istanbul), 12 (20 July 1967), 34–35.

Izzettin, Kasim. *Hicaz'da Teşkilat ve Islahat-i Sıhhiye ve 1329 Senesi Hacc-i Şerif*. Istanbul: Matbaa-i amire, 1328/1910.

Jaussen, Antonin. *Coutumes des Arabes au pays de Moab*. Paris: Lecoffre, 1908.

————, and Raphael Savignon. *Mission archéologique en Arabie (Mars-Mai 1907)*. Paris: Leroux, 1909–22.

"Kayfiyyah jamaʾa iʾanah sikkah hadid al-Hijaz." *Al-Manar*, 6 (1903), 355.

Kazem Zadeh, Hossein. *Rélation d'un pèlerinage à la Mecque en 1910–1911*. Paris: Leroux, 1912.

Keddie, Nikki R. *An Islamic Response to Imperialism: Political and Religious Writings of Sayyid Jamal ad-din "Al-Afghani."* Berkeley: Univ. of California Press, 1968.

————. "Pan-Islam as Proto-Nationalism." *Journal of Modern History*, 41 (1969), 17–28.

————. *Sayyid Jamal ad-Din "al-Afghani": A Political Biography*. Berkeley: Univ. of California Press, 1972.

Kedourie, Elie. "The Surrender of Medina." *Middle Eastern Studies*, 13 (1977), 124–43.

"Khatt al-hadid al-hijazi." *Al-Manar*, 3 (1900), 283–85.

Kıcıman, Naci. *Medine Müdafaası Yahut Hicaz Bizden Nasıl Ayrıldı?* Istanbul: Sebil Yayınevi, 1971.

Kinross, John Patrick Balfour, Baron. *Ataturk: The Rebirth of a Nation*. New York: Charles Scribner's Sons, 1964.

Kurd ʾAli, Muhammad. *Kitab khitat al-Sham*, 6 vols. Damascus: Al-Matbaʾat al-Taraqqi, 1925–1928.

————. "Sikkat al-Hijaz." *Al-Muqtataf*, 29 (1904), 970–80.

Landau, Jacob M. *The Hejaz Railway and the Muslim Pilgrimage: A Case of Ottoman Political Propaganda*. Detroit: Wayne State Univ. Press, 1971.

Lawrence, T. E. *Seven Pillars of Wisdom*. Garden City, N.Y.: Doubleday, 1935.

McMunn, George F., and Cyril Falls. *Military Operations: Egypt and Palestine from the Outbreak of the War to June 1917*. London: H.M.S.O., 1928.

———. *Military Operations: Egypt and Palestine from June 1917 to the End of the War*. London: H.M.S.O., 1930.

Al-Madi, Munib, and Sulayman Musa. *Tarikh al-Urdunn fi al-qarn al-ʾishrin*. Amman: N.p., 1959.

Al-Marawani, Ahmad. *Al-Khatt al-hadidi al-hijazi*. Damascus: Damascus Univ., 1959.

Mousa, Suleiman, *T. E. Lawrence: An Arab View*. London: Oxford Univ. Press, 1966.

Musa, Sulayman. *Al-Husayn ibn ʾAli wa al-thrawrat al-ʾarabiyyat al-kubra*. Amman: Dar al-Nashr, 1957.

———. *Suwar min al-butulah*. Amman: Al-Matbaʾat al-Hashimiyyah, 1968.

Musil, Alois. *The Northern Hegaz: A Topographical Itinerary*. New York: American Geographical Society, 1926.

———. *Northern Negd: A Topographical Itinerary*. New York: American Geographical Society, 1928.

Ochsenwald, William. "Ottoman Subsidies to the Hijaz, 1877–1886." *International Journal of Middle Eastern Studies*, 6 (1975), 300–307.

———. "The Financial Basis of Ottoman Rule in the Hijaz, 1840–1877." In William Haddad and William Ochsenwald, eds., *Nationalism in a Non-National State: The Dissolution of the Ottoman Empire*. Columbus: Ohio State Univ. Press, 1977, pp. 129–49.

———"The Jidda Massacre of 1858." *Middle Eastern Studies*, 13 (1977), 314–26.

———. "Muslim-European Conflict in the Hijaz: The Slave Trade Controversy, 1840–1895." *Middle Eastern Studies*, in press.

Ottoman Empire. Administration Sanitaire. *Mouvement général et statistique comparative par pavillon de la navigation dans les ports ottomans*. Constantinople: Haim, 1914.

Peake, Frederick G. *A History of Jordan and Its Tribes*. Coral Gables, Fla.: Univ. of Miami Press, 1958.

Pepper, Charles M. *Report on Trade Conditions in Asiatic Turkey*. Washington, D.C.: Government Printing Office, 1907.

Philby, H. St. J. *The Land of Midian*. London: Ernest Benn, 1957.

Pinon, René. *L'Europe et l'Empire Ottoman*. Paris: Perrin, 1909.

Pönicke, Herbert. "Heinrich August Meissner-Pascha und der Bau der Hedschas- und Bagdadbahn." *Die Welt als Geschichte*. 16 (1956), 196–210.

Quataert, Donald. "Ottoman Reform and Agriculture in Anatolia, 1876–1908." Diss., Univ. of California, Los Angeles, 1973.

Ralli, Augustus. *Christians at Mecca*. London: Heinemann, 1909.

Rambert, Louis. *Notes et impressions de Turquie: l'Empire Ottoman sous Abdul-Hamid*. Geneva: Ator, 1926.

Rey, Alexis. *Statistique des principaux résultats de l'exploitation des chemins de fer de l'Empire Ottoman*. Constantinople: N.p., 1896–1913.

Rida, Muhammad Rashid. "Mahabbat Allah wa rasulihi fi i'anat al-sikkat al-hadidiyyat al-hijaziyyah." *Al-Manar*, 3 (1900), 361–64.

Rifaat. *Rapport général sur la campagne du pèlerinage de 1909, au lazaret de Tèbuk*. Constantinople: Gérard Frères, 1909.

Roloff, Max. "Arabien und seine Bedeutung für die Erstarkung des Osmanen Reiches." *Länder und Volker der Türkei*, 5 (1915), 113–36.

Saliba, Najib. "Wilayat Suriyya, 1876–1909." Diss., Michigan, 1971.

Schmidt, Hermann. *Das Eisenbahnwesen in der asiatischen Türkei*. Berlin: Siemenroth, 1914.

Shaw, Stanford J., and Ezel Kural Shaw. *History of the Ottoman Empire and Modern Turkey*. 2 vols. Cambridge: Cambridge Univ. Press, 1977.

Shorrock, William. *French Imperialism in the Middle East: The Failure of Policy in Syria and Lebanon, 1900–1914*. Madison: Univ. of Wisconsin Press, 1976.

"Sikkah hadid al-Hijaz." *Al-Hilal*, 13 (1904), 187.

"Sikkah hadid al-Hijaz." *Al-Muqtataf*, 25 (1900), 95.

"Sikkah hadid al-Hijaz wa daribah laha jadidah." *Al-Manar*, 5 (1903), 877.

"Sikkat al-hadid al-hijaziyya." *Al-Manar*, 25 (1924), 200–205.

Slemman, H. [Lammens, Henri]. "Le chemin de fer de Damas–La Mecque." *Revue de l'Orient Chrétien*, 5 (1900), 507–34.

———. "Où en est le chemin de fer La Mecque." *Revue de l'Orient Chrétien*, 6 (1901), 145–52.

Stékoulis, C. *Le pèlerinage de la Mecque et le Choléra au Hedjaz*. Constantinople: De Castro, 1883.

Stitt, George. *A Prince of Arabia—The Emir Shereef Ali Haidar*. London: Allen and Unwin, 1940.

Sykes, Mark. *The Caliphs' Last Heritage*. London: Macmillan, 1915.

"Taqrir hawla al-wad' al-shar'i li al-khatt al-hadidi al-hijazi." Mimeographed. Damascus, 1964.

Thamarat al-Funun. Beirut, 1898–1908.

Tibawi, A. L. *A Modern History of Syria, Including Lebanon and Palestine*. London: Macmillan, 1969.

Tignor, Robert. *Modernization and British Colonial Rule in Egypt, 1882–1914*. Princeton: Princeton Univ. Press, 1966.

Toukan, Baha id-Din. *A Short History of Trans-Jordan*. London: Luzac, 1945.

Toydemir, Sait. "Hicaz Demiryolu İnşaatı Tarihinden." *Demiryollar Dergisi*, 22 (1948), 65–68.

Tresse, René. *Le pèlerinage syrien aux villes saintes de l'Islam.* Paris: Chaumette, 1937.

United Arab Republic. Directorate General of the Hijaz Railroad. "Résumé of the stages of the entry of the Hijaz Railroad into participation in the hot mineral springs" Mimeographed, Damascus, 1960. (in Arabic).

Uzunçarşılı, Ismail H. *Mekke-i Mükerreme Emirleri.* Ankara: Türk Tarih Kurumu Basımevi, 1972.

Wavell, A. J. *A Modern Pilgrimage to Mecca.* London: Constable, 1918.

Wiedenfeld, Kurt. *Die deutsch-türkischen Wirtschaftsbeziehungen und ihre Entwicklungsmöglichkeiten.* Munich: Duncker, 1915.

Wilson, Samuel G. *Modern Movements among Moslems.* New York: Fleming Revell, 1916.

Wirth, Albrecht. *Vorderasien und Aegypten in historischer und politischer, kultureller und wirtschaftlicher hinsicht geschildert.* Stuttgart: Union Deutsche, 1916.

Young, George, comp. *Corps de droit Ottoman.* 7 vols. Oxford: Clarendon Press, 1905.

Zeine, Zeine N. *The Emergence of Arab Nationalism.* Beirut: Khayat's, 1966.

Zihni Paşa. *Beyan-i hakikat.* Istanbul: Ahmet Ihsan, 1327/1909.

Zolondek, Leon. "*Al-Ahram* and Westernization: Socio-Political Thought of Bisharah Taqla (1853–1901)." *Die Welt des Islams*, 12 (1969), 182–95.

INDEX